Loretta Santini

POMPEII

AND THE VILLA OF THE MYSTERIES

Published and printed by

NARNI – TERNI

Photographs: Archivio Plurigraf - Amendola - Bianchi e Sperandei - Dal Magro - Jodice - Barone - Laura Ronchi - Atlantide - Marka - Il Dagherrotipo - Sie
Aerial photos authorization S.M.A. n. 506 del 20 - 6 - 91
© Copyright by Casa Editrice Plurigraf
S.S. Flaminia, km 90 - 05035 Narni - Terni - Italia
Tel. 0744 / 715946 - Fax 0744 / 722540 - (Italy country code: +39)
Printed: 2000 - Plurigraf S.p.A. - Narni

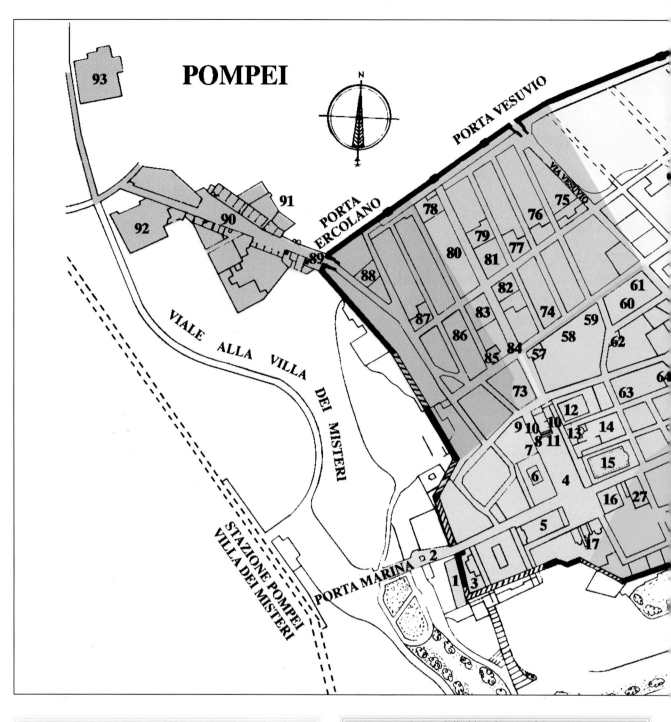

POMPEI

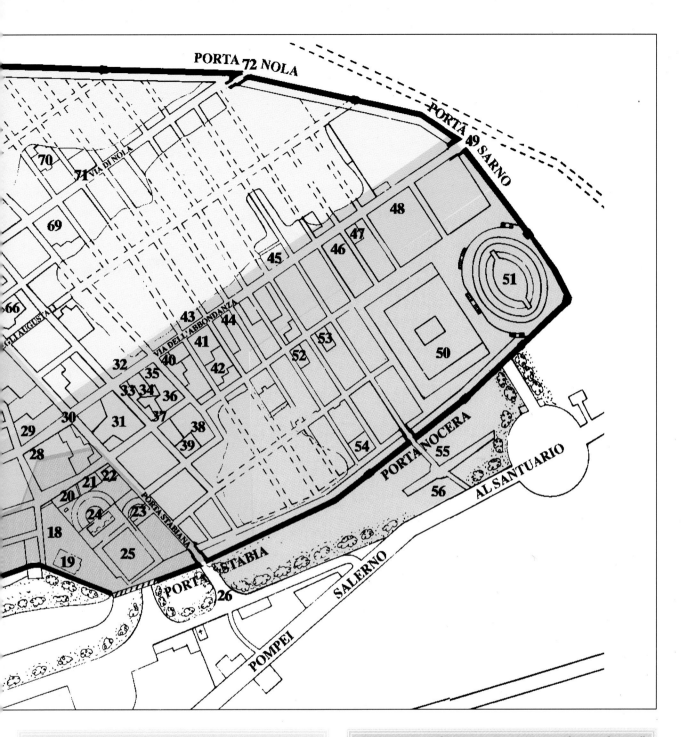

REMINDERS OF THE PAST AND THE FASCINATION OF THE EXCAVATED CITY

Pompeii is one of the most significant proofs of Roman civilization and, like an open book, provides outstanding information on the art, customs, trades and everyday life of the past.

The city has re-emerged from the darkness of centuries precisely as it would have been when it was unexpectedly buried in the thick layer of ash and lava which poured down from the devastating eruption of Vesuvius. It was the year 79 A.D. The scale of the tragedy was appalling: in what had been one of the most active and splendid Roman centres, life came to a permanent standstill. The thick layer of volcanic material which submerged it, made up to a large extent of ash and lapilli - non-hard material, unlike that which covered Herculaneum and which solidified into extremely hard stone -has meant that the city has remained intact until the present day, not only as far as its buildings are concerned, but also as regards the contents inside the houses and shops, providing an absolutely fascinating picture of *"daily"* life.

The walls of the houses are covered with electoral propaganda messages or risqué jokes aimed at particular citizens. The signs on the shop doorways indicate the activity carried out there or the name of the owner. Alongside the elegant villas belonging to the nobility and the luxurious residences of the middle class, stand modest houses where several families lived. The peasant dwellings on the other hand are situated around vegetable gardens or small plots of land. On the edge of the city stood the brothels, squalid rooms intended as places of pleasure for sailors and travellers passing through.

In the narrow lanes, the workshops and utility rooms provide further evidence of the daily routine performed by workmen and slaves as well as the women of the house.

Panoramic view of the archaeological area of Pompeii.

The houses still contain furniture, ornaments, gold and silverware, work tools, kitchenware, bronze and terracotta lamps, foodstuffs of all kinds, counters for serving drinks, grain mills and grindstones, workshops for manufacturing cloth, smithies and outlets selling groceries, fruit and vegetables.

There is a remarkable record of Roman painting, of which, without the finds made in Pompeii, virtually nothing would be known. The architecture and development of the various types of houses is also amply documented.

Thus the excavated city provides outstanding historical evidence of Roman civilization: these reminders of the past, which are so vivid and tangible in the remains brought to light, contribute to the fascination of the present.

HISTORICAL OUTLINE

Pompeii, unlike the other towns in Campania founded for the most part by Greek colonists, was built by the Oscans, probably around the 9-8th century B.C., even if the evidence now available does not go back beyond the 6th century.

The town developed on lava terracing formed many centuries earlier. It constituted an important natural defence against the threat of invasion by neighbouring peoples. At the same time the volcanic nature of the land meant the territory of

the Sarno valley was particularly fertile, thereby allowing for the rapid development of the agricultural economy.

Pompeii soon made contact with the nearby Greek colonies, whose culture, way of life and the religion of Magna Graecia it quickly absorbed. Evidence of this is to be found in the shape of the Doric temple which stands in the Triangular Forum.

The city was subject to the Etruscans for almost fifty years (until 474 B.C.) when the latter occupied part of inland Campania. Immediately afterwards it came back under the Greek sphere of influence. It then became part of the Samnite area of expansion (5th century), under whom it saw remarkable growth, forming that historical centre whose remains are still visible. This can be

identified in part of the most ancient boundary wall, in the architecture of several houses (those characterised by a Tuscan-type atrium), in the public buildings in the Triangular Forum and in the Temple of Apollo in the Civic Forum.

Meanwhile Rome had begun its gradual advance towards southern Italy and had started to overcome the resistance of the Italic peoples. As a consequence even the Samnites were forced to surrender to the Eternal City, though only after three long and bitter wars, the last of which was fought in the years between 298 and 290 B.C. As a result of the conquest of Campania, Pompeii also ended up under Roman dominion, becoming an "associate", a status which allowed for the maintenance of a relative local autonomy.

From that time on its history was closely connected with that of the Eternal City and only on the occasion of the social war waged by the Italic peoples in a final attempt to defend their freedom, did it ally itself with the insurrectionary movement (91 B.C.). In 89 B.C., however, it was besieged by Sulla, taken by storm and thus brought back under the aegis of Rome. In 80 B.C. it became a Roman colony with the name of *Colonia Cornelia Veneria Pompei*.

As in the past, Pompeii continued to expand and develop in every sector, in the economic field in particular, greatly helped by its fertile hinterland and its advantageous position.

All the activities linked to trade and maritime traffic saw a period of growth. This remarkable development had immediate results: outside, it led to an increase in the level of prestige of Pompeii compared with other Campanian towns; within, as a consequence of growing wealth, there was a general increase in the standard of living for many of the social classes. As a result the "middle-class", that is to say the class of merchants and entrepreneurs who had built Pompeii's fortune and had reaped their reward, was able to establish itself in an increasingly prominent way.

Pompeii's flourishing economy led to a decisive population increase, widespread affluence and in addition the remarkable embellishment of the town. It is true to say that the middle-class derived great pleasure from competing with the nobility in the construction of splendid villas. The nouveaux riches, in their desire to outdo the aristocratic class who traditionally held power, vied in displaying their own wealth through the opulence of their houses and the preciousness of their ornaments and jewellery.

The urban building expansion took place for the most part along Via dell'Abbondanza, a symbolic centre of the new emerging class.

However, the life and splendour of Pompeii was destined to come to an end. The first inklings of the tragedy were felt in about 62 A.D., when a violent earthquake devastated the city and the surrounding countryside.

It was no mean feat to recover from this blow. The least well-off class suffered the most serious consequences, having seen their houses destroyed. Most of the public and private buildings were still at the strengthening and restoration stage when Vesuvius became active, and in the space of a few hours sowed death and destruction on the city. It was the 24th August in the year 79 A.D. A heavy shower of ash, lapilli and lava from the volcano began to rain down onto the city and onto nearby Herculaneum and Stabiae. All was buried beneath a thick blanket of volcanic material to a depth of several metres. The inhabitants, who for the most part fled in the direction of the coast, were suffocated by the fumes of the gases, others met death in their own homes.

GENERAL APPEARANCE OF THE CITY

Pompeii shows the typical topography of a Roman city with its decuman and cardinal roads (the principal thoroughfares) which intersect at right angles creating an orthogonal grid: the **cardo** follows a north-south direction, the *decumanus* lies east-west.

The principal axes consist of Via di Nola - the major decuman road - and Via Stabiana (the main cardinal road).

With the expansion of the city, two other streets were added to support the urbanistic layout and run almost parallel to the former: these are Via dell'Abbondanza, which became the town's new main decuman road, and the Via del Foro, which wound its way parallel to Via Stabiana to make a second cardinal road. Both were linked to the large civic Forum, and constituted the centre of the town's political and economic life.

Two important crossroads - the Orpheus crossroads and the Holconius crossroads - were the junctions for the main axes in Pompeii. Around these axes a close network of streets sprang up, which served to mark off entire blocks of houses (*insulae*).

The urban centre, with the exception of the **Forum** area, which lies on a flat piece of land, is characterized by a remarkable difference in level caused by the lava terracing which spread across the lower slopes of the mountain.

The layout of the city is rectangular in form. Around it runs the elliptical perimeter of the **walls** which extend for about 3 km along the edge of the basaltic terracing: several stretches date back to the Samnite era, others to the expansion which took place in the Roman age. Various **gates** open into the defensive boundary wall: their names are Marina, Ercolano, Vesuvio, Nocera, Capua and Sarno.

The most ancient centre in Pompeii is the part massed around the Triangular Forum. The new Forum, on

Pompeii excavations: overall view of the city. In the foreground the Large Theatre, the Odeon and Via Stabiana are visible.

the other hand, was built in the vicinity of Porta Marina out of the centre, when the city, which by now had increased remarkably, felt the need for a larger space.

The **Theatre, the Amphitheatre** and the **Gymnasium** were built in the peripheral area. **Thermal Baths** were set up in several parts of the city so that they might answer more adequately the needs of the citizens by serving the various urban areas. Outside each gate a large **burial ground** with sepulchral monuments grew up.

As evidence of the city's enormous urbanistic expansion, a vast urbanized peripheral area was discovered outside Porta di Ercolano: it contains houses, workshops and superb **villas** such as that of Diomedes and the Villa of the Mysteries. Another of the suburban villas which characterized the period of maximum expansion of Pompeii is the one located in the vicinity of Porta Marina, known as the suburban villa of Porta Marina.

The **houses** can be dated back to various historical periods: those belonging to the pre-Samnite period are simpler in their layout and almost always made of tuff; those of the Samnite period are more elaborate; without doubt those from the Roman age show the greatest degree of perfection.

The **temples** in Pompeii are concentrated in the area of the large Forum and the Triangular Forum and reproduce traditional Greek designs.

Plentiful examples of workshops can be found throughout the city: there are numerous **fullonicae** (places for the treatment of cloth), a fundamental sector in Pompeii's economy, to the extent that the Dyers' Guild had its own building in the Forum (the so-called Building of Eumachia) containing shops and warehouses for the storage of goods.

There are a good many "**thermopolia**", that is refreshment rooms (the equivalent of modern-day bars), in-

tended for the serving of drinks and recognizable from the counters with holes in them used to hold amphorae. In addition we find **bakeries** and **mills**, often attached to warehouses for storing grain.

In general all the workshops are adjacent to the house of their owner, thus making it more convenient for him to do his job and allowing him to involve his entire family and servants in the enterprise as well.

Pompeii had a supply of **hotels** and rooms to let: several buildings bear inscriptions which are advertisements for leases. Private **baths** were also frequently let out. Furthermore there were plenty of **gambling dens** and houses of pleasure **(lupanari)**.

Among the curiosities worthy of note are the **pedestrian crossings** located at the road junctions: these consist of very large stones placed crosswise along the streets: people were able to walk on them and so avoid getting their feet wet in case of rain.

Casa dei Casti Amanti (House of the Chaste Lovers): Example of excavation work inside the stall.

Aerial view of a Pompeian house.

Attention is due to the **signs** on the shops, often in the form of painted pictures and depicting the activity carried out there and the name of the owner.

The walls of the houses are dotted with **inscriptions**: these are public announcements of performances or advertisements for rooms to let, as well as electoral propaganda messages and words of a lewd nature referring to various people or situations.

THE TEMPLES

Roman temples - the ones in Pompeii in particular - do not diverge in any way from the great Hellenistic models known through the colonies of Magna Graecia.

The main nucleus was provided by a cella (naos) - where the statue of the god was housed - enclosed in a larger structure usually rectangular in shape.

The latter varied in its structure according to the arrangement of the colonnade: the temple with columns incorporated in the central front part was called in antis, that with the whole front opening onto a colonnade was known as prostyle; that with columns placed at front and back was called amphiprostyle; the temple with a ring of columns around its entire perimeter was peripteral and that whose perimeter was surrounded by a double colonnade was dipteral.

The shape of the capitals gave rise to a further distinction in three orders: Doric, Ionic and Corinthian according to whether they were completely flattened, had two side volutes or were decorated with acanthus leaves.

THE HOUSE

There is ample documentation of the Roman house in Pompeii, from modest dwellings to large and magnificent villas with sumptuous decorations, from simple workmen's houses to the elegant residences of the noble class, from the homes of merchants which were built around their workshops, to those with their own vegetable garden and plots of land used for agricultural purposes.

The typical house is variable in size and has a rectangular plan. It is almost totally devoid of windows on the outside, since all the rooms face onto the inner courtyards.

Typical house of the first period: "Tuscan" atrium: the entrance or **vestibulum**, often closed off by a wooden door, gave access to the **atrium**. This was covered by a sloping roof **(compluvium)** open in such a way as to channel rainwater into the **impluvium**. In subsequent periods it was known as **tetrastyle**, because it was embellished with four columns which held up the impluvium. Around this room ran a colonnade and a series of rooms known as **cubicula**, which were the family's sleeping quarters.

The atrium was followed by the **tablinium** (meeting and reception room) and the **triclinium** or dining room. The garden opened onto the back of the house and was surrounded by a colonnade or **peristylium**. The latter, adopted from Hellenistic models, was the result of the transformation of the old kitchen garden (several villas had a garden as well as a vegetable patch) and led to the expansion of the residence and to the creation of rooms used for receiving guests **(oecus)**.

At the back of the house were the **kitchens** and **storehouses**. With the passing of time the house greatly increases in terms of size, the spaces and rooms being doubled, to the point that it occupies almost an entire insula. At the same time it becomes particularly refined and pays special attention to embellishments and elegant decorations.

With the gradual development of the middle-class, the model house saw further modifications dictated by the new needs of the resident families. First and foremost, workshops were added in which the owner could carry out his activity. The apartment lay at the back of these and above and, in most houses, is linked to the rest by staircases and accessways.

In this case the house shows a more simplified plan, since part of the space was taken up by the workshops.

THERMAL BATHS

The "thermae" were the city's public baths. There were relatively few private baths and these were limited to the most well-to-do families, given that the latter were the only ones who could afford to build rooms suited to the purpose.

The thermal bath buildings were divided into two sections: one reserved for women and one reserved for men. Each of these contained a series of rooms with different functions:

1) **apodyterium** or changing room
2) **frigidarium** or cold bath room
3) **tepidarium** or tepid bath room
4) **calidarium** or hot bath room.

The thermal baths included **latrines** and, in the most developed type, a **pool** and **gymnasium**. They were often furnished with open spaces and gardens.

The system of heating the rooms - which was fairly ingenious -worked by running heated water through the cavities in the wall.

The Thermae were not only buildings used for a function of public utility, but also played a very important social role in that they provided an important place for people to meet.

THEATRE

The theatre was the place where performances of comedies and tragedies were held.

It included a semi-circular **cavea** from which led the series of steps divided into sections on which the spectators sat. Below was the area for the **orchestra** (the part intended for the chorus) and the **scena**, that is the stage where the actors performed.

The theatre in Pompeii shows the features of Greek models in that it exploits the natural inclination of the terrain. The Roman-type theatre on the other hand depends on an architectural structure.

Aerial view of the area around the Stabian Thermal Baths.

Amphitheatre: built on the outskirts of Pompeii in '80 B.C. at the command of the magistrates Quintus Valgus and Marcus Porcius, it probably represents the prototype for buildings of this kind.

AMPHITHEATRE

It is presumed that the amphitheatre in Pompeii, the oldest known to us, must have provided the basic model for the subsequent buildings. The form derives from the duplication of the structure of the theatre (amphitheatre means "double theatre" or "circular theatre"): it is an elliptical structure situated in a depression in the ground and backing onto embankments.

It consists of a large **cavea** around which are the steps, divided into sections, which cover the entire perimeter of the construction. The various sections of the cavea - ima cavea (*low part*), media cavea, (*middle part*) and summa cavea (*upper part*) - were intended for the various social classes: the seats in the lower central area were reserved for dignitaries, while those high up were for the plebeians. It was furnished with accessways to the seats as well as with entrances to the cavea. The amphitheatres were sometimes equipped with a velarium (*a large canopy which was stretched over the amphitheatre in case of rain*) and, in the more developed types, with a system of canals and bulkheads which allowed the cavea to be flooded so that naval battles could be staged.

PAINTING

Before the discovery of Pompeii, information about Roman painting was scarce and fragmentary with rare examples limited to fragments of frescos found in isolated cases. The discovery of the city, with its rich pictorial heritage, has, however, allowed for a new debate to be opened on the whole issue of Roman art. On the basis of the studies carried out and the classification made by Vitruvio, the paintings are usually divided into 4 styles:

I style: known as "incrustation" or "structural" style. It was commonplace between the 2nd century and the middle of the 1st century B.C. It is a simple and bare style of painting: through the use of plaster and colours in which black, yellow and red predominate, it tends to imitate marble panels.

II style: it lasted until the middle of the 1st century A.D. It is known as architecture in perspective or simply architectural since, as well as faking marble facings, it reproduces colonnades, arches and buildings seen in perspective. The result is an imaginary space with increasing or decreasing effects. The great cycle of the Mysteries in the villa of the same name belongs to this period. At its most advanced stage, glimpses of the countryside are painted between the imaginary buildings.

III style: is called "real painting" and belongs to the 1st century A.D. It sees a return to a simpler style in terms of the layout and stroke. The background becomes flat and is rendered with a single colour: the figures are embellished and the decorative elements accentuated. The painting of the III style is also known as "Egyptianizing" in that the ornamentation often recalls ancient Egyptian motifs.

IV style: is known as "architectural illusionism" or "ornamental". Its characteristics recall the painting of the second period, but the composition becomes increasingly exaggerated and unreal. It almost seems as if there was an attempt to extend the walls through the creation of imaginary spaces. The decoration becomes, so to speak, baroquesque: the houses are filled with stuccos and overloaded with ornamentation, usually in demonstration of the opulent state achieved by the resident families. Friezes and festoons are abandoned.

MOSAICS

Mosaic ornamentation was widely used in the decoration of the houses in Pompeii and saw various stages of development.
The oldest examples are works executed with simple motifs, using tesserae of rough workmanship and of modest material; those of subsequent epochs, on the other hand, show refinement in their composition, in their taste in colour and in the preciousness of the tesserae used. In the first period the works are characterized by the repetition of simple geometric motifs or they repeat the pictorial patterns of the second, third and fourth phases. Mosaics were often used as flooring. There are some admirable examples: the famous "cave canem" placed at the entrance to many houses is perhaps the best-known among the many which have survived. The panel depicting "The Battle of Alexander"

housed in the Archaeological Museum in Naples and originating from the House of

the Faun, is, though, one of the most important and magnificent examples.

Opposite: *depiction of Achilles and Chiron, fresco housed in the Archaeological Museum in Naples.*
Above: *several examples of the mosaic art in Pompeii: the tragic masks which decorate the House of the Faun.*
Below: House of the Wild Boar: *a hunting scene.*

SCULPTURE

The sculptures which have survived show that in Pompeii there was a preference for statues of a small size, given that they were designed for ornamental purposes, to be incorporated into rooms and gardens, to embellish fountains, atria or tablinia. The large statues, those that is which had a commemorative function, were for the most part situated in the Forum. The favoured material was bronze, although there are plenty of small masterpieces in marble, tuff and terracotta. "The dancing Faun", the "Drunken Silenus" and the "Wild boar under attack" are some of the pieces which combine with the freshness and immediacy of their design an exquisite workmanship. A special mention should be given to the "Doryphorus", a beautiful copy of a splendid Greek sculpture. There are various fragments of statues originating for the most part from the area of the Forum and from the temples dedicated to the Capitoline Triad.

INSCRIPTIONS AND GRAFFITI

The walls of the houses in Pompeii are frequently covered with **inscriptions**: these are electoral propaganda messages which urge the citizens to vote for one or other of the candidates. At times an entire category of workers (goldsmiths, marble-cutters, bakers, blacksmiths) holds the candidacy. At other times an aspiring magistrate puts himself forward to the people for a particular office. They are written in red or in black and for the most part in capital letters. They were executed by the professional scribes who also dealt with official communications, the sentences of the tribunal, the buying and selling of slaves and public decisions. There are around three thousand electoral inscriptions in Pompeii and most of them can be dated to the city's final year of existence, given that it was customary to rub out the old inscriptions to make way for new ones. The **graffiti**, on the other hand, are the messages which were made by scratching on the walls of the houses: these relate to the most disparate subjects and paint an extremely vivid and frank picture of contemporary social life: they include risqué jokes, comments on a particular person or event, caricatures of famous people, reflections on love, as well as appreciative remarks about a beautiful woman or the pleasure experienced in the privacy of one of the rooms in the brothel. In addition there are several which are concerned with the buying and selling of materials or livestock and the calculation of merchandise. Many refer to the entertainments on offer in the city or are in praise of the champions put to the test in the gladiatorial games.

Opposite: Apollo shooting arrows: bronze statue originating from the Temple of Apollo.
Above: Examples of Pompeian sculpture housed in the Archaeological Museum in Naples: the dancing Faun (originating from the House of the Faun) and the Ephebus (originating from the House of the Ephebus).

I SUBURBAN VILLA OF PORTA MARINA

It stands by the boundary wall outside Porta Marina: it was at one time linked to the latter by a passageway which led from the garden. It is situated in a delightful position with extensive views overlooking the sea. The construction is of the early 1st century. Of this only a few ruins remain, but the impression received is one of a grandiose and magnificently designed house. In fact the building, which is incorporated into the fortification walls and close to the lava terracing on which the city stands, exploited the difference in level of the terrain by extending over several storeys. A large portion of the magnificent colonnade can still be admired, which, with its Corinthian columns and fine plaster decorations, must have been outstandingly beautiful. The triclinium too, part of whose structure is still standing and which is perhaps one of the largest rooms found in Pompeii, provides the modern-day visitor with a marvellous example of refined decoration belonging for the most part to the III style. In particular, depictions of "**Theseus**", of "**Daedalus and Icarus**", of the "**Minotaur**" and numerous others can be seen - there are several portraits of *poets* set in panels in the upper part - which should be appreciated for their delicate and skilful craftsmanship. Of interest is the decoration which characterizes the surviving walls of other rooms, such as the small pictures with a *mythological subject* which decorate one of the cubicula in the triclinium, or those with the depictions of the "**Satyr and Bacchante**" placed in the second triclinium. The suburban villa came to light as a consequence of the bombings in the last world war.

2 PORTA MARINA

This is the main entrance to the Pompeii excavations and takes its name from its seaward-facing position. It stands on the western side of the boundary wall. At one time it bore the name of Porta Neptunia and, notwithstanding its vicinity to the area of the Forum, was never the preferred access of the Pompeians, given that it opened onto a stretch of very steep and uneven terrain, making it somewhat inconvenient. The gate consists of two barrel arches: one, the more awkward, was used for the transit of beasts of burden, the other for pedestrians.

3 ANTIQUARIUM

The Museum, set up to house some of the finds made in the archaeological area of Pompeii (the others

Porta Marina: opening onto the western side of Pompeii, it provides access to the archaeological site.

have to a large extent been transferred to the National Archaeological Museum in Naples) and in particular the documentation concerning the history of the excavations, was reorganized and almost completely rebuilt after the bombing suffered during the last world war. Its various rooms house materials and collections from the necropolises in the Sarno valley, which can therefore be dated back to the Campanian civilizations: terracottas, bronzes, parts of temple decorations and buccheri. One of the rooms houses exhibits from the Samnite epoch. Of great importance are the *capitals* made of tuff, the material most widely used at that time, and belonging to several buildings in the Samnite centre. Among the most interesting and most effective in terms of the strength of their depiction are the *capital of the house of Torellus* and those from the so-called house of the Capitals, for the most part depicting *Maenads and Satyrs*. There are some interesting bas-reliefs of several *metopes* which were part of the Doric Temple in the Triangular Forum: the one which portrays the *"myth of Ixion"* is particularly beautiful. There is a remarkable *pediment* and *altar* from the Temple of Sant'Abbondio, belonging to the Dionysian cult, as it is possible to infer from the subject of the bas-reliefs which portray *Dionysus and Ariadne*. The Roman age is strongly represented by several finds among which the statue of *"Livia"* stands out, a beautiful portrait of the woman found in the Villa of the Mysteries. The depiction of the empress was connected with the domestic cult and with the personification of the Roman *pietas*. Also worthy of mention is the precious and refined *"portrait of Marcellus"*.

The Museum, alongside the works of greatest artistic importance, exhibits small statues, amphorae, cups, vases and a vast collection of materials which offer a panoramic view of the objects in most common use and the furnishings belonging to the houses in the Roman age: earthenware, bronzes, bone needles, necklaces, small glass amphorae and silverware of various kinds. In addition it houses a dra-

View of Mount Vesuvius seen from the amphitheater.

matic collection of several of the so-called "impressions", that is the plaster casts of people and animals taken by surprise during the volcanic eruption. Particular attention should be paid to the section which exhibits the remains of foodstuffs preserved beneath the ashes. Last but not least the Antiquarium hous-

es the busts of all those who contributed to bringing this city to light. Next to Porta Marina stood the **Temple of the Pompeian Venus** (the tutelary deity of the city) of which few traces remain -the platform on which it stood can still be recognised - after its destruction in the earthquake of 62 A.D.

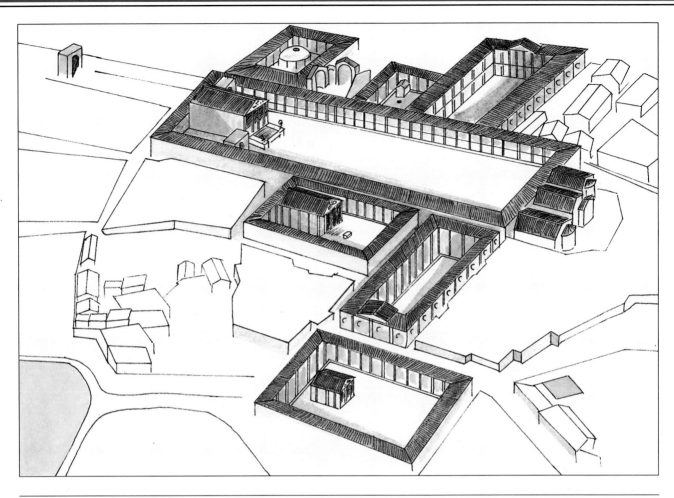

Reconstruction of the Forum.
Following page: View of the Temple of Apollo.

4 THE FORUM

This was the ideal centre of the city, providing a religious nucleus (the main temples stood here, such as the ones dedicated to Jupiter, father of all the gods, Apollo and the Lares) and a political axis, in that it was here that justice was administered and the town's public institutions were situated. In addition it was the economic heart of the city, the place where bargaining and commercial transactions took place. It was also the site of the storehouses for foodstuffs and, in some cases, of the headquarters of the most representative categories of workers. The Forum was a vast square usually situated in a central position. The one in Pompeii, which consists of a large rectangular area of more than 400 metres in perimeter, is situated in the south-western section and therefore decentralized compared with the inhabited centre. The choice of the area was determined, among other factors, by the need to find an area which would be big and level enough, which given Pompeii's situation on lava terracing was no mean feat.

In the subsequent age the Civic Forum grew up on the site of the older and more central Triangular Forum, although there were plenty of buildings in the area dating back to the Samnite epoch, such as the Temple of Apollo. This happened when, owing to changing socio-economic conditions, the marked population increase and the constant urbanistic expansion, it became necessary to create a new public space which could answer more adequately the changing needs of the population and the dignity of the city itself. As a consequence the area which until the 2nd century B.C. had been set aside for the town market was now utilized. The Forum in Pompeii stands at the junction of the town's main roads, the Via dell'Abbondanza in particular, which was the most important centre of the prosperous Roman city. The remains of this important social meeting place show only in part the majesty and the beauty of one time. The image which the Forum once projected was undoubtedly far more magnificent and monumental: it is enough to consider that the square used to be surrounded on three sides by a long and elegant colonnade which in its turn was surmounted by an airy open gallery. Between the columns stood statues of illustrious personages as well as the dais set aside for orators. At the far end rose the flight of steps of the Capitolium or Temple of Jupiter which spectacularly closed off the fourth side of the square.

PLAN OF THE IMPERIAL FORUM

5   Basilica
6   Temple of Apollo
7   Mensa Ponderaria
8   Horrea and Forum Olitorium
9   Public Latrines
10 Honorary Arches
11 Temple of Jupiter
12 Macellum
13 Temple of the Lares
14 Temple of Vespasian
15 Building of Eumachia
16 Comitium
17 Office of the Duumviri

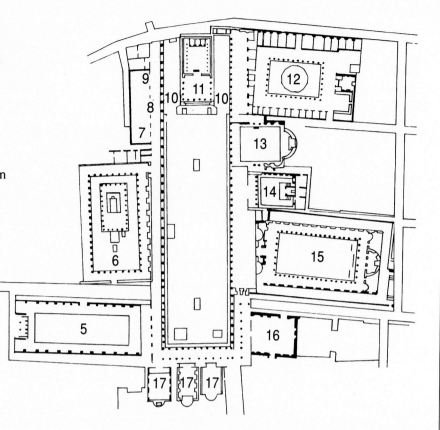

Previous pages: *panoramic view of the Forum area. The square covers an area of 38 x 142 m.*
Aerial view of the Pompeii excavations.

The Forum: The Basilica.

The Forum: The Temple of Jove.

Above: View of the Forum, the political, trade and religious center of the city.
Below: Honorary arch built next to the Temple of Jove and view of part of the Forum.

Antiquarium: The museum was built to house some of the artifacts found in the archeological area of Pompeii.

THE COLONNADE

It runs round three sides of the Forum (the fourth, the north side, is occupied by the Temple of Jupiter). The oldest part is the southern part: it was executed in the Samnite epoch and the material used was tuff. The colonnade and the trabeation of the western and eastern sections on the other hand are made of travertine marble and should be attributed to the Roman age. The open gallery which ran above the arcade was made up of soaring columns: part of it can still be made out on the western side. Between the columns of the colonnade were numerous sculptures dedicated to illustrious personages: today only some of their pedestals remain.

THE BUILDINGS IN THE FORUM

5 BASILICA

A magnificent building, monumental in its proportions and importance. It represented the nucleus of the Forum in that it was here that the public life of the town was centred. The construction is preceded by a colonnade and consists of a large rectangular room divided lengthwise by a series of columns (there are 28) into three naves. A row of semi-columns leant against the walls. At the back of the building was the raised area set aside for the tribunal, distinguished by two orders of columns placed in front. Access could be gained to it by two flights of stairs. The parts still visible today bear witness to the elegance and the balanced architectural design of the complex. The Basilica was probably executed around the 2nd century B.C. (this can be inferred from the inscriptions and several factory marks imprinted on the tiles). Some experts, on the basis of the discovery of several tiles and on the study of the position of the columns, have speculated that the building may have been covered by a roof, whilst others maintain that the central nave must have been trabeated and open to the sky.

Forum: interior of the Basilica. The building, of vast proportions (55 x 24 m.), was the ideal centre of public town life. Opposite: Reconstruction of the Basilica.

The **Basilica** in ancient Rome was the place set aside for the administration of justice (Tribunal) as well as being the building where contracts of various kinds were stipulated and legalized. In the more ancient temples, at the dawning of Greek civilization, it was the seat of the king (in Greek "basileus" meant "king") and therefore the place which symbolized the maximum level of power. When, as a result of changing political conditions, it ceased to be the seat of a sovereign, it became the place set aside for the administration of judicial power, continuing to play a role of the greatest importance throughout the imperial age. With the fall of the empire and after the arrival of Christianity, the building, with all its architectural features and together with the name which distinguishes it, became the place where religious functions were performed: all the Catholic churches and the early Christian ones in particular were called "basilicas" as a result and had the same plan and the same structure as the Roman model.

6 TEMPLE OF APOLLO

It is an integral part of the Forum area even though it predates it. It goes back, at least as far as its primitive nucleus is concerned, to the 6th century, that is to the Samnite period. It was then extended, the part which jutted out into the Forum square being closed off and embellished around the 1st century A.D., particularly under the Emperor Nero. The building shows architectural features of both Italic and Greek derivation and has a rectangular plan with the perimeter being surrounded by an astonishing 48 columns. The inner cella, raised on a podium, was reached by means of a long flight of steps. Opposite these was the sacrificial altar.

The central part, which contains the altar to the god, is also surrounded by columns. It is adorned with two statues depicting "**Apollo shooting arrows**" and "**Diana**" (the originals are housed in the National Archaeological Museum in Naples). On one of the columns which mark off the cella of the god there was a sundial.

7 MENSA PONDERARIA

Weights and measures were examined in this building to ensure they were uniform with the official Roman units.

8 HORREA AND FORUM OLITORIUM

These were the storerooms for foodstuffs and later provided a market for herbs and cereals. Two of the rooms may have been used as an **Aerarium**, that is the State Treasury. At the front of the Horrea stand eight large brick pillars.

9 PUBLIC LATRINES

These were situated behind the horrea and the Temple of Jupiter.

10 HONORARY ARCHES

Between the Horrea and the Temple of Jupiter stands the **arch of Drusus**: at one time covered in marble, the bare brick structure is all that remains. A twin honorary arch used to stand on the other side of the Temple. It was demolished to allow for a better view of the **arch of Tiberius** or Germanicus which stands behind and provides access to the square from the central Via del Foro.

Temple of Apollo: it was built in the 6th century B.C. and transformed and embellished at the same time as the Forum was constructed. Reconstruction of the Temple of Apollo.

Above: *overall view of the Temple of Apollo.*
Opposite: *the Macellum, a building of the imperial age used as the town market.*

11 TEMPLE OF JUPITER OR CAPITOLIUM

This was the main centre of religious life in Pompeii. Situated on the northern side of the Forum, it is dedicated to the highest divinity of ancient times - actually it was built in honour of the Jupter, Juno and Minerva triad - and towers above a wide staircase with two large arches either side which have remained virtually intact. In a spectacular manner it closed off the fourth side of the square where there was no colonnade.

The temple, dating back to the 2nd century B.C., was built in two stages, the second of which, scheduled towards the end of the same century, led to the expansion of the architectural structure.

The building shows at the front the remains of some tall fluted columns: these also continued along the sides as far as the cella which is spacious and fairly elongated.

The large "**head of Jupiter**" found here is in the Archaeological Museum in Naples.

The building was seriously damaged by the earthquake of 62 A.D. and, at the moment of the eruption of 79 A.D., it had not yet been restored to its original splendour.

12 MACELLUM

This was the name of the city market. It dates back to the 1st century A.D., is square in shape and was preceded by a wide colonnade beneath which were the entrances to retail outlets.

The Macellum had three entrances, one of which, the main one, was furnished with an aedicule. Inside the building were more "**tabernae**" (shops), while in the centre was an aedicule with a dome resting on twelve columns set above a tank full of water.

This was probably the part used for the fish market, a theory supported by the discovery of fragments of fish bones in the drainage canal.

Of particular interest is what remains of a marvellous painting which adorned the back wall of the building.

Some of the numerous statues which embellished the construction have also been found in the macellum.

13 TEMPLE OF THE LARES

This sanctuary was dedicated to the protector gods of the house and

was built by the Pompeians as a token of their gratitude for having escaped the perilous earthquake. Executed in brick, it has a rectangular plan enlivened at the far end by an apse with fine ornamental columns and with niches either side.

The Lares were the tutelary deities of the house and were probably to be identified with the deceased: they protected the property and the family. Each house had a site or a small temple dedicated to them.

14 TEMPLE OF VESPASIAN

This is a small cult building of which part of the façade of the outer structure still remains - the side walls are decorated with blind gabled windows - and a cella raised on a pedestal. The latter, standing on a podium, was at one time preceded by four fluted columns supporting a pediment. Opposite is an altar in marble decorated with bas-reliefs depicting *"sacrificial scenes"*

15 BUILDING OF EUMACHIA

Built during the reign of the Emperor Tiberius, it was commissioned by the priestess Eumachia to accommodate the guild of *"fullones"* or launderers and dyers of cloth, a category whose importance was such that it could afford to have its principal headquarters in the economic and social heart of the city. In terms of its proportions this building is inferior only to the Basilica. At the front is a colonnade above which unfurls a dedicatory inscription to the priestess. Worthy of note is the magnificent **portal** characterized by an elegant decoration of acanthus leaves. Inside was a spacious colonnade which followed the perimeter of the courtyard and which ended at the back in three apses, one of which housed the statue of **"Concordia"** personified in the figure of Livia, wife of the Emperor Augustus. At the back, on the other hand, was a corridor, or cryptoporticus, probably used for the storage of cloth which was then sold in the open space of the courtyard. Here stood the statue dedicated to *Eumachia.*

16 COMITIUM

This was a public space used for electoral purposes. Voting was carried out here for the elections of the Pompeian magistrates.

17 MUNICIPAL OFFICES

These three buildings occupy the southern side of the Forum. Each was used for dealing with the paperwork and the services related to the ranks of the *duoviri*, the *edili* and the *decurioni*.

The buildings are virtually identical. The central one was probably the Archive and was furnished with shelves, as can be inferred from the space created by the pillars which demarcate the inner walls.

*The **duoviri**: the most important office in the city. The former fulfilled a role similar to that of the consuls and had a mainly judicial function.*

*The **decurioni** were the representatives of the town senate.*

*The **edili** supervised the running of public services.*

Opposite: *Remains of the Temple of Jove and imaginary reconstruction.*
Below: *colonnade of the Edificio di Eumachia (Building of Eumachia).*
Photos on the following pages: *Altar of the Temple of Vespasian (Forum) and reconstruction of the entire place of worship.*

Example of a Pompeian house.

Above: **Building of Eumachia: aerial view of the whole.**
Below: **Bas-reliefs from the dorway to the Edificio di Eumachia (Buildin of Eumachia).**
Opposite: *a glimpse of the colonnade which closes off the Forum area.*

II Itinerary: The Triangular Forum and the Area of the Temples and Theatres

18 Triangular Forum - 19 Doric Temple - 20 Samnite Gymnasium - 21 Temple of Isis - 22 Temple of Jupiter Meilichios
23 Small Theatre or Odeon - 24 Large Theatre - 25 Gladiators' Barracks - 26 Porta di Stabia.

The VIII region occupies the southwest part of Pompeii and consequently the area of Porta Marina, Porta Stabia and the Holconius crossroads. It includes the area of the Triangular Forum and part of the buildings situated in the stretch of Via dell'Abbondanza between the Holconius crossroads and the Civic Forum. (*Via dell'Abbondanza, see itinerary no.*3) This is the ancient heart of Pompeii, given that it is massed around the area of the original Forum - known as Triangular because of its shape, - the nucleus of the social, political and economic life of the town before it became one of the most important and rich commercial centres in the area and saw a significant rise in the population and a strong urbanistic development. Characteristic of this area is the irregular nature of the terrain which had a marked influence on the layout of the streets and the structure of the houses. Indeed the whole of the VIII region stands on steeply sloping ground, being on the extreme edge of the lava terracing on which the city was founded. For this reason the streets never show that tendency towards an orthogonal grid typical of Roman town planning and the houses, in order to adapt to the natural difference in level, are often spread out over two storeys and their architectural design enlivened by open galleries and access stairways. The area is situated in the southern part of Pompeii and lies between Via dell'Abbondanza and Via delle Scuole.

18 TRIANGULAR FORUM

The name derives from the square's triangular shape. The outer edge reaches as far as the confines of the lava terracing and consequently looks out over the plain below. As

One of the buildings in the Triangular Forum.
Opposite: *view of a part of the Triangular Forum. So-called owing to its characteristic shape, it was the primitive nucleus of the town.*

mentioned above, the Triangular Forum represents the original social and political centre of Pompeii, and as a result can be said to belong to the Samnite epoch. The entrance is made up of **Propylaea** characterised by a fine colonnade of Ionic type. There is a fountain adjacent. The inside of the square is bordered by another colonnade of Doric type - there are an astonishing 95 columns - while one side of it has a panoramic view towards the sea. In all likelihood the colonnade was originally used for gymnastic activities. In the centre of the area stands the Doric Temple, and consequently the **sacred area** which extends around the temple itself, with **three altars** in tuff from the

pre-Roman age and a **sacred well**. The pedestal standing in front of the entrance supported the *statue of M. Claudius Marcellus*, nephew of the Emperor Augustus.

19 DORIC TEMPLE

This is among the oldest in the city and probably dates back to the 6th century B.C.: it was dedicated to the cult of Hercules who, tradition has it, was the founder of the city. Subsequently the goddess Minerva was worshipped there too. The pedestal and the staircase which gave access to it are all that remain of the building. Otherwise there are only fragments which belong to the renovation work which the temples

underwent: column drums and fragments of capitals. The terracotta decorations which were part of the high fascia of the Temple are housed in the Antiquarium.

20 SAMNITE GYMNASIUM

Constructed in the Samnite epoch it was the centre for the gymnastic activities of the Pompeian nobility until the time of the creation of the much larger gymnasium situated on the outskirts of the city near the Amphitheatre. It has a rectangular plan bounded on three sides by a colonnade and is surrounded by high walls. Its proportions were reduced at the time of the construction of the Temple of Isis. The archi-

tectural layout is extremely plain. It was here that the beautiful statue of the "**Doryphorus**" (lance bearer) was found, now housed in the National Archaeological Museum and which represents one of the masterpieces of ancient art. It is a copy of the more famous statue by the Greek sculptor Polycleitus.

21 TEMPLE OF ISIS

This is a real jewel of Greek architecture and one of the best preserved buildings in Pompeii. An inscription informs us that the temple was restored in order to remedy the damage suffered as a consequence of the earthquake of 62 A.D.: this has certainly contributed to its present state of preservation, as can also be said for the beautiful pictorial decoration which has now been removed and is housed in the Archaeological Museum in Naples. The building consists of a large rectangular space marked off by walls, within which is the cella of the god raised up on a pedestal and standing in a splendid niche. Of interest and great elegance is the **small temple** - with its plaster decorations - situated in the peristyle and used for the preservation of the Nile water considered to be holy by the members of the cult of the Egyptian goddess Isis. Adjacent to the temple there is also a space to accommodate the priests' houses and for the meeting of the faithful.

22 TEMPLE OF JUPITER MEILICHIOS

This rather small building became the principal seat of the cult of Jupiter and the Capitoline triad Jupiter-Juno-Minerva, when the larger temple of Jupiter on the Forum square was destroyed in the earthquake of 62 A.D. Fragments of the statue of the lord of Olympus were found among these very ruins. It is adorned with a large tuffaceous altar.

Above: *Triangular Forum: the Temple of Isis, one of the most elegant monuments in Pompeii.*
Opposite: *reconstruction of the Temple of Isis.*

Mime was a special theatrical performance of a comical or even bawdy nature, inspired by aspects and incidents of everyday life. Usually it only lasted for a short time.

The actors used masks as a rule and women were also admitted to the performance, which was not otherwise the case.

Mime originated as farce in Sicily and was later modified in the Roman age.

Above: *bas-relief statue (telamon) situated in the cavea.*
Below and opposite: *the Odeon and the Large Theatre.*

23 SMALL THEATRE OR ODEON

Established in the 1st century B.C., it represents one of the most harmonious and well-balanced examples of architecture of this type. It could hold up to 1,000 spectators and could be covered permanently. It is well preserved and shows the typical design of the Greek theatre with its structure deeply embanked in the natural slope of the terrain. It was used to host plays and musical events. In addition it was used for the performance of mimes.

24 LARGE THEATRE

This is a magnificent building constructed in the 2nd century B.C., with the stage area subsequently undergoing conversion. As a type it conforms to the Greek theatres in that the architectural structure adapts to the natural inclination of the terrain. During performances it could be covered, but it was not equipped with a permanent canopy, a privilege enjoyed by the Small Theatre. It had a remarkable capacity, being able to hold up to 5,000 spectators. Comedies and tragedies were acted here. A special feature of this theatre was the natural background which could be used as scenery: there is in fact a panoramic view across to the splendid ring of mountains which stand behind Pompeii. In the southern area of the Theatre there was a colonnade set aside to accommodate the spectators during the intervals or at the end of the performance.

25 GLADIATORS' BARRACKS

This very ancient building was closely connected with the Theatre, since originally it provided a meeting place for the audience in the intervals during the performances. Under Emperor Nero it was used as the gladiators' barracks, a suitable place for providing accommodation and a practice area for those men who were employed to fight. It has a square plan preceded by an entrance and columns. Around the perimeter runs a colonnade of 74 columns. It consists of two floors and includes in addition, storehouses, dining rooms and sleeping quarters. The numerous weapons found during the excavation work are housed in the Archaeological Museum in Naples and provide extensive documentation of great interest.

26 PORTA DI STABIA

Its name derives from the fact that it connected Pompeii with Stabiae. Set into the ancient and mighty walls and providing an opening in the southern stretch, it is perhaps the oldest gate in the city. The deep imprints left on the paving of the street which passes through it bear witness to the heavy traffic with which it had to contend. On its far side is the beginning of the Via dei Sepolcri.

View of the Gladiators' Barracks and the quadriportico which bounded the area of the building.
Opposite: the Via Stabiana starts from the Porta di Stabia and crosses the city perpendicularly as far as Via dell'Abbondanza.

VIA DELL'ABBONDANZA

The Via dell'Abbondanza, even though it was built at a later date than the other thoroughfares in the town, soon came to constitute the city's main road and the place where the new emerging class developed those commercial activities which were to make Pompeii one of the most important centres in Campania. This circumstance was at the root of the great changes which took place within Pompeian society and in particular provided the opportunity for an immense urbanistic development. A highly significant factor in this evolution was the growing needs of the population and above all the wish of the emerging wealthy class to build itself houses suited to its new social status, thereby seeking to equal and even to better, in terms of luxury and size, the villas of the nobility. Along the Via dell'Abbondanza numerous workshops sprang up and, joined to these, the houses of their owners. The design of these houses responds to different criteria from those of the classical-type house. In fact they consist of a complex of rooms ranged over at least two floors so that commercial activity could be carried out on the ground floor, with the upper floor being set aside for family life, but in such a way that the two were closely linked and all the members of the household could comply with the necessary demands of work in the most functional way possible.

The houses in this area are often furnished with jutting out roofs, terraces and accessways.

View of the Via dell'Abbondanza, the main thoroughfare of Pompeii: most of the city's commercial activities developed along this street.

Via dell'Abbondanza is one of the principal decuman roads of the city: one end of it leads to the area of the civic Forum and the other to the area of the Amphitheatre, crossing Pompeii in a south-west, north-east direction. Its name derives from the sign placed on the **Fountain of the Holconius Crossroads** which depicts a *cornucopia*, the symbol of plenty.

27 HOUSE OF
THE WILD BOAR

This house contains the remains of some very interesting mosaics. Particularly worthy of mention is the one which gives the house its name and which, placed on the floor of the atrium, depicts a hunting scene showing a *"wild boar assailed by dogs"*. There is also a precious mosaic decoration distinguished by geometric motifs. The marble floors and the area around the garden are of immense beauty.

Above: *reconstruction of the Via dell'Abbondanza.*
Below: *mosaic floor from the House of the Wild Boar.*

Detail of the head and horn of plenty on the Fountain of Abundance: this has given its name to the main thoroughfare in Pompeii.

28 HOUSE OF HOLCONIUS RUFUS

Previous pages:
Details of Pompeian streets: pedestrian passages consisted of large stone slabs placed crosswise.
Opposite: Amphorae, earthenware, various finds and impressions.
Partial view of the Stabian Thermal Baths.

It belonged to one of Augustus' tribunes, a prestigious personage of the age. The house is spacious and elegant. The remains allow us to guess at the architectural structure, which must have been particularly beautiful in the area of the tablinium and the peristyle characterized by an airy open gallery. Precious pictorial decoration covered a large part of the walls of the house. Of additional interest would have been the summer triclinium, adorned with fountains and a cycle of paintings. The frescos, which must once have been splendid, are now only partly visible as a result of deterioration: they depict *"mythological scenes and characters"*

29 STABIAN THERMAL BATHS

These occupy a vast area between the Brothel lane, the Holconius crossroads and the Via Stabiana. They represent the oldest thermal complex in the city. In fact they were built at the time of Pompeii's subjugation to Rome and were subsequently extended and decorated on more than one occasion to answer more adequately the needs of the growing population.

The original construction, situated in the northern part of the building beyond the colonnades, is from the Samnite period. The more recent part - dating back to the renovation of the Roman age - overlooks the western side: it is organized according to more modern and functional criteria.

The thermal complex consists of a well-constructed system of baths distributed around a central area used as a gymnasium and characterized by a colonnade ranged round three sides of the building.

The Stabian Baths are composed of three parts: the rooms in the north section, those mentioned above as being the oldest, contain a series of latrines. The second section consists of a group of private baths situated behind the northern colonnade. The third section is located in the eastern part: it is made up of changing rooms, a vestibule - with magnificent plaster decoration - rooms for the cold bath (*frigidarium*), for the tepid bath (*tepidarium*) and for the hot bath (*calidarium*).

The Thermal Baths are rigidly divided between the area set aside for men and the area set aside for women. Both are organized in the same way, but the female section is more simple and less decorated.

A pool occupies the western side of the Baths.

The rooms are frequently adorned with stuccos of fine workmanship and certainly among the most beautiful in Pompeian art.

It is also possible to identify the system used to heat and cool the various rooms, which was achieved by pipes carrying air and water of varying temperature through the cavities in the walls.

In the third section the public baths are equipped with a pool and rooms used for practising gymnastic activities.

Below: *one of the many impressions which bear witness to the tragic end of the inhabitants of Pompeii.*
Opposite: *interior of the Stabian Thermal Baths.*

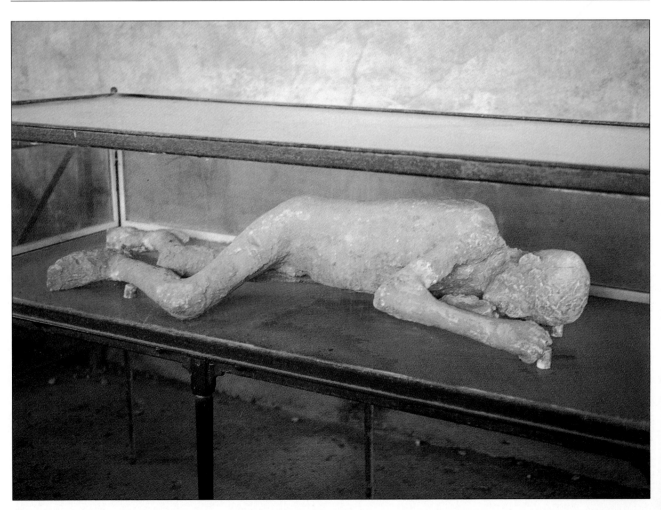

30 HOLCONIUS CROSSROADS

This represents the junction point of the major Pompeian thoroughfares, that is the Via dell'Abbondanza and the Via Stabiana. The name derives from the statue of Holconius Rufus, an illustrious personage of the town, which at one time was placed at the base of the arch which stood here. On one of the corners is a **Fountain** bearing the symbol of the *Concordia Augusta*.

Above: *detail of the interior of the Thermal Baths: the frigidarium.*
Below: *a section of the courtyard in the thermal bath building.*
Opposite: *a thermopolium, the place from which drinks were served.*

31 HOUSE OF THE CITHARIST

This is one of the largest houses in Pompeii and is made up several houses merged into one. The name derives from the statue depicting "**Apollo the citharist**" found here and housed in the Archaeological Museum in Naples, as is the very fine mosaic showing a "**Wild Boar assailed by dogs**".

Notwithstanding the fairly poor state of preservation, this house allows us to guess at the magnificence of the architecture of the interiors and the richness of the decorations which once made it splendid. Of great spectacular effect are the three superimposed peristyles.

32 HOUSE AND WORKSHOP OF VERECUNDUS

This complex is of the greatest interest in that it provides an example of a typical workshop belonging to the sellers and dyers of cloth, an activity which in Pompeii was particularly well developed and so renowned that a building in the Forum square was dedicated to them, the Building of Eumachia. Precious paintings embellish the workshop and depict the activity carried out there and the protector gods. Note in particular: "*Mercury with a moneybag*", "*Venus on a carriage*", "*The cloth sellers*" and "*The weaving of cloth*". They are all depicted with great immediacy.

Inside of a workshop with machines for grinding corn.

THE WORKSHOPS

Pompeii provides ample documentation on the type of workshops which existed in ancient times and consequently on the various activities carried out in the town.

There are the **fullonicae**, which are the workshops of the textile workers (see Fullonica Stephani and the series of rooms in ins. 6, nos.6-12, whose interiors contain all the working tools and the tanks used for dy-ing and manufacturing cloth); the **thermopolia**, that is to say the equivalent of modern-day bars with counters for serving drinks. There are a good many **tabernae** which correspond to the inns of today.

Bakeries are widely represented, equipped with mills for grinding grain, as are bread-makers' **(pistrinum)**, **warehouses** for storage and counters for the sale of bread. There are also plenty of outlets selling fruit and vegetables and garum, the latter being one of the favourite sauces of ancient times, as well as workshops belonging to the cloth, wood and iron craftsmen. In general all the shops bear **insignia** on the façade of the place itself, showing the symbol of the owner's category or trade; inscriptions and graffiti are frequently found, which not only indicate the name of the workshop, but also provide a list of materials and notes on the merchandise.

33 HOUSE OF CASCA LONGUS

The group of workshops which occupy part of insula no.6, belong to a single owner, a certain Casca Longus who had his house built in close communication with the shop. On the walls of the atrium a delightful decoration showing scenes related to the theatre can be admired, and in one of the rooms, another one with *floral motifs*. The house owes its name to the inscription borne by the trapezophori, that is the statues which support the table, and probably belonged to that Casca Longus who was one of the protagonists in the conspiracy which led to the assassination of Caesar.

34 FULLONICA STEPHANI

This is one of the best preserved workshops in Pompeii. The fullonicae were the laundries. Observation of the interior of the workshop allows us to reconstruct all the stages of the treatment of cloth, from washing, to pressing, to drying and dying. The Fullonica Stephani (Stephanus was the owner's name) contained a spacious room to accommodate customers.

Fullonica Stephani: this was a workshop used for the treatment of cloth.

THE TREATMENT OF CLOTH

The cloth was first immersed in large washing vats where it remained for some time together with substances which helped to remove the grease (urine and soda). Next it was put into other vats where it was rubbed and trampled underfoot.

In the following stage the cloth was softened by the use of special clays, then trampled again and immersed once more in basins of water to remove any impurities it may have accumulated.

The cloth was finally carded, shaven, dyed and stretched in special presses.

35 HOUSE OF THE LARARIUM

A room near the tablinium and commonly known as the Lararium shows refined decoration with depictions of "*scenes from the Iliad*". The blue colouring of the background is interesting and creates an intensely atmospheric effect. There is a large painting in the so-called Hall of the Elephants. From an examination of the plastered walls and the material found in the rooms, we can infer that, at the moment of the catastrophic tragedy, the house was in the process of being decorated.

36 HOUSE OF THE CRYPTOPORTICUS

It takes its name from the cryptoporticus - a room of startling effect thanks to apertures which allow shafts of light to filter in - which was the underground cellar of the house used for storing wine. It contains an exhibition of plaster casts of people who died during the eruption of Vesuvius. The house also contains pictorial decoration related to the II style. It consists of **Episodes taken from the Iliad** incorporated into a frieze (in the colonnade). In addition there are some admirable caryatids painted in red and *still lives*.

37 HOUSE OF LUCIUS CEIUS SECUNDUS OR HOUSE OF THE CEII

The house stands along the lane which leads off to the right from Via dell'Abbondanza. Its name can be inferred from the electoral inscriptions found on the front of the house. This dwelling is distinguished by the panelled decoration on the façade. It has a precious tetrastyle atrium. Inside there are several ornaments and some furniture - particularly noteworthy is the cast made of the **wardrobe** - as well as the staircase which joined the ground floor to the top floor. In the garden a delightful picture depicting *animals and plants* can be admired.

38 HOUSE OF MENANDER

This is one of the largest and most elegant houses in Pompeii, very rich in its decoration and highly complex in the division of the rooms. Its name derives from the portrait of Menander, but is it also known as the "*house of the silverware*" because of the copious collection of pieces found in a chest in

The peristyle of the House of Menander, one of the most elegant houses in Pompeii.
Opposite: Atrium of the House of Menander. Notice the small votive Temple by the side of the entrance.

the cellars of the house: a total of 118 pieces of silver as well as numerous others made of gold and coins. The house belonged to the Poppei family and underwent various building phases. Begun in the 3rd century B.C., it was later extended and embellished; at the moment of the eruption of Vesuvius the building works were still underway. From the entrance - distinguished by two pillars with Corinthian capitals - access could be gained to the atrium (of Tuscan type), which is fairly well preserved and atmospheric as a result of the decoration in the IV style, the charming little temple placed in one corner and above all because it preserves intact its jutting out wooden roof open at the centre to allow light to pass through and to facilitate the collection of water. The rooms to the left of the entrance contain paintings showing scenes taken from **Episodes of the Iliad**. Beyond the tablinium is the peristyle, an elegant and refined room with its beautiful painted colonnade. A series of rooms leads off from here: on the right is the kitchen and bathroom area; on the left is the triclinium flanked by two rooms with frescoed walls. The exedrae situated beyond the rooms set aside as servant accommodation contain refined paintings of a mythological and theatrical nature (masks) and the portrait of the **poet Menander** mentioned above. The western area of the house is occupied by the quarters set aside for use as bathrooms: there is a fine calidarium whose mosaic and pictorial decoration is virtually intact. One section of the house was reserved for the curator of the property, a freedman called Eros (we have learnt his name from the seal found on his body), who safeguarded the goods in the house and who bore the title of Procurator.

Above: Interior of the Casa del Menandro (House of Menandrus): detail of the bath.
Below: Casa degli Amanti (The Lovers' House): the fresco for which the villa was named.

39 HOUSE OF THE LOVERS

This house, albeit of modest proportions, is an architectural jewel. The decoration of the walls shows great refinement and the peristyle surrounded by a double open gallery is truly delightful. The ceilings and floors of several of the rooms are intact. In the atrium is a collection of friezes, panels and painted medallions. The name of the house derives from an inscription which refers to the sweetness of love and states that "lovers, like bees, wish life to be as sweet as honey".

40 HOUSE OF PAQUIUS PROCULUS

Paquius Proculus was a highly influential political figure in Pompeii.

This complex structure underwent various phases of construction. The mosaic decoration in the atrium with geometric panels depicting animals is very elegant. The tablinium has a fine alabaster floor. The pictorial decoration has partially survived and shows the remains of some "**still lives**". Several skeletons of children were found in this house.

41 HOUSE OF THE PRIEST AMANDUS

In the fine triclinium is an admirable series of paintings with a mythological subject: "**Hercules**", "**Polyphemus**", "**Perseus**" and "**Daedalus and Icarus**". A painting of the pre-Roman epoch can also be found near the entrance. There is a noteworthy plaster cast of a **tree** in the garden of the peristyle.

42 HOUSE OF THE EPHEBUS

It takes its name from the statue of the **Ephebus**, a bronze copy of a similar Greek work of the 5th century B.C., found here and transported to the Museum in Naples.
It is a very large house and sumptuous both in terms of its architectural design (it consists of three houses merged into one), and in the decoration which characterises it. This confirms that it belonged to a family of the rich middle-class who were keen on an ostentatious display of their high standard of living.
Of the paintings preserved here, that of "**Venus and Mars**" is worthy of mention. The marble covering of the floors is quite remarkable - the one in the triclinium is particularly precious in that it was executed with rather rare coloured marble - as is

Casa degli Amanti (The Lovers' House): Archaeological excavations.

that of several walls. Among the objects found here are four statuettes - the *placentarii* - which were used as sauce boats and which are characterized by their provocative nature (Museum in Naples). Worthy of attention is the small house connected to the former where some outstanding paintings embellish the tablinium, having as their subject "**The marriage of Venus and Mars**".

43 THERMOPOLIUM OF ASELLINA

The Thermopolia were the places where drinks were sold. The one named after Asellina - one of the names written on the plaster on the walls - is perhaps the best preserved in Pompeii: apart from the stone counters with holes in to hold the amphorae for pouring drinks, it preserves ornaments, containers for hot drinks and a good many bronze vases. The names of the women written on the walls of the workshop and the presence, on the upper floor, of numerous small rooms, has led to the assumption that the owner of the thermopolium ran another business as well, perhaps not just a mere sideline, which consisted of managing a house of pleasure.

44 HOUSE OF THE ORCHARD

It owes its name to the pictorial decoration showing "**Trees and fruit**" which adorns some of the rooms, one of which has a blue background and one black. They are paintings of extreme freshness and refined elegance.

Several types of trees (fig, plum, cherry, arbutus and lemon) are faithfully reproduced; in the fascia below, a delightful garden is depicted. Some experts have connected these paintings with the Dionysian cult; others, more simply,

Thermopolium of Asellina: view of the counter which held the amphorae for serving drinks.

House of the Orchard: details of the pictorial decoration with naturalistic subjects.

have imagined that the owner was a fruit-grower.

45 HOUSE OF TREBIUS VALENS

The name of the owner can be inferred from an inscription in the bedroom. Its façade was once covered by inscriptions which almost certainly served as public announcements. Inside is an admirable peristyle with an unusual pictorial decoration of geometric motifs and a triclinium furnished with fountains and a pergola. One bedroom contained a collection of small bottles for ointments and jewels, which leads to the supposition that the room belonged to the owner's wife.

46 HOUSE OF LOREIUS TIBURTINUS

The house underwent two phases of construction: the first relates to the area within the Tuscan atrium (Samnite epoch); the second, centred around the peristyle area, is to be attributed to the imperial age. The house is distinguished by its magnificent garden consisting of an open gallery and a pergola embellished by water channels, fountains and a temple as well as by pictorial decorations and sculptures. The **mythological depictions** bear the signature of their author, a certain Lucius. Precious paintings adorn the triclinium (**Episodes from the Iliad**). Other paintings, for the most part belonging to the IV style, decorate one of the small rooms next to the large hall. An interesting feature is provided by the cast made of the great entrance **portal** to the house. The combination of the decoration and the architectural layout of this house bear witness to the prestige and affluence of the family who lived there.

House of Loreius Tiburtinus
Above: *the garden with the open gallery and the pergola.*
Below: *scenes with a mythological subject: Narcissus at the spring and Pyramus and Thisbe.*
Opposite: *detail of the niche flanked by frescos with a mythological subject.*

47 HOUSE OF VENUS

This was the residence of a well-to-do family, as can be inferred from the richness of the materials used and from the decorations. Apart from the fresco depiction of *"doves, fountains and flowers"*, there is a remarkable large fresco of *"**Venus in a sea-shell**"* on the garden wall. The scene is delightful in appearance: the Goddess is ploughing through the waves in a shell escorted by Cupids. The fresco is peopled with birds and flowers. On one side is a depiction of the god *"**Mars with weapons**"*. Other rooms contain paintings including the particularly fine ones on a black background.

House of Venus: the garden wall (photo below) shows "Mars" (photo above), "Venus on a seashell with Cupids" (photo above right) and "Naturalistic scenes" (photo below right).

48 VILLA OF JULIA.FELIX

This is a magnificent construction and occupies the whole of insula no.4: it consists of a villa, a thermal complex given over to public use and a collection of workshops merged into one.

The house proper, furnished with two entrances, is spacious and luxurious. At one time it was adorned with paintings, though these have now been removed and are housed in the Louvre Museum. The garden enlivened by fountains, bridges and columns is highly atmospheric. In the triclinium the beds are made of marble and the bath complex is furnished with every comfort - frigidarium, tepidarium, calidarium and also a sauna facility - it is laid out according to the typical public bath design and also includes an outdoor pool. Initially it belonged strictly to the villa, but was later given over to public use upon payment of a fee, as demonstrated by an inscription to this effect found here. The complex of workshops and rooms situated along the lane to the west was also created by the landlady with the intention of leasing them out.

A vast area lies at the back of the villa, set aside for the cultivation of fruit and vegetables.

49 PORTA DI SARNO

It was constructed in the Samnite epoch and is now in a somewhat deteriorated condition.

On the right lies the vast area on which the Large Gymnasium and the Amphitheatre stand.

House of Julia Felix: the garden area with the colonnade with fluted columns.

50 LARGE GYMNASIUM

It was established in the 1st century A.D. when, owing to the sharp population increase and the great urbanistic development which overtook Pompeii, the Samnite Gymnasium situated in the Forum proved insufficient. It consists of a majestic colonnade of quadrangular shape including a large space intended for the practice of gymnastic specialities. It also contained a pool.

51 AMPHITHEATRE

This is an impressive and grandiose construction, capable of holding up to 12,000 spectators (others have calculated 20,000). It hosted all the circus shows and the gladiatorial games so dear to the Pompeians, who devoted most of their spare time to these performances.
The period of its construction dates back to 80 B.C. (it was commissioned by the magistrates Quintus Valgus and Marcus Porcius) and is therefore one of the oldest buildings in existence, which leads to the inference that it might have represented a model for all those which were subsequently built in Rome.
It was constructed in part by making use of an embankment, in part by digging down into the earth for several metres. The access steps are outside the building. The doors on the western side lead into the arena.
Unlike the other Roman amphitheatres, the one in Pompeii does not have an underground section. It was equipped with a *velarium*, that is a cover which was stretched over the complex in case of rain: the rings to which the canopy was fixed can still be seen.

The Large Gymnasium: a large space used for gymnastic exercises.

52 THERMOPOLIUM OF THE PHOENIX

Unlike the other thermopolia in Pompeii, this one has extremely modest features and consists essentially of a place of refreshment situated in the shade of a simple pergola. The location takes its name from the depiction of the *phoenix* depicted on the shop sign. Alongside it two *peacocks* are also painted.

53 GARUM WORKSHOP

This is none other than a sauce factory, to be precise the "garum" which was much used and appreciated in ancient times. The containers for its preservation can still be seen.

54 GARDEN OF THE FUGITIVES

Its name derives from the garden in which many corpses of Pompeians were found, seized by death as they were about to flee from the

garum
This is a sauce made from eggs and the innards of various fish. These were chopped, salted and allowed to ferment in baskets with holes in, so that the liquid could filter through. It was one of the favourite foods of the Romans and was used as a basic condiment for a number of dishes.

city. Their "**impressions**" have been left in situ where they were found. The corpses of the thirteen victims thus provide one of the most vivid and terrible proofs of the disaster. The land was joined to a type of farm-house.

55 PORTA NOCERA

This was constructed in the pre-Roman age and then rebuilt at later dates. It opens up in the southern stretch of the walls of Pompeii, along the uneven lava spur which makes access particularly awkward.

56 NECROPOLISES

The vast area occupied by the cemetery was partly brought to light only a short time ago. The tombs are numerous and of various types: worthy of particular mention are the *sepulchre of Eumachia*, that of the *Gens Tillia* and that of *Serapius*, a Pompeian banker.
In addition the *tomb of the duovir Cellius* and the truly monumental one of *Agrestinus Equitius* can be identified, commissioned for the latter by his consort Veia Barchilla.

Aerial view of Vesuvius and the archaeological area with the Amphitheatre in the foreground.

Tombs of Porta Nocera: the necropolis extends for a long way beyond the perimeter of the city walls.
The bodies found in the Garden of the Fugitives, a dramatic proof of the tragedy which struck Pompeii with the eruption of Vesuvius.

THE IMPRESSIONS

These provide dramatic evidence of the city's last living moments. They take the form of casts of people, animals, objects, furniture and even plants, obtained by pouring liquid plaster into the space left in the ground by the disintegration of the solid matter. Their conception was inspired by Fiorelli, one of the originators of the excavation of Pompeii. He realized that as the corpses and objects had decomposed, they had left a vacuum in the ground. This "vacuum" was carefully cleaned of any residual matter and filled with plaster, which, once set, perfectly assumed the shape of whatever had lain beneath the ashes. After the procedure was finished, the "impressions" were brought to light. The result was a collection of realistic and dreadful images captured in the moment of their demise: the terror-stricken expressions on the faces of the people are haunting, as are the suffocated cries on their mouths. Several of the corpses were caught in the act of embracing one another, almost as if to stave off the calamity; some were caught as they were trying to flee; others were surprised in the act of rescuing valuable objects and money from the cataclysm.

The neighbourhoods situated east of the Forum form the central nucleus of Pompeii.

They lie between Via del Foro, Via della Fortuna as far as the Orpheus Crossroads, Via Stabiana as far as the Holconius Crossroads and Via dell'Abbondanza, which stretches between the latter and the Civic Forum.

The urban conglomeration is fairly irregular as a result of the differing level in the lie of the land. This itinerary passes through small and winding streets such as **vicolo Stor-** to, one of the most characteristic and atmospheric in Pompeii, with houses and workshops backing on to one another, almost fighting over the small amount of space available.

57 TEMPLE OF FORTUNA AUGUSTA

It was built in the 1st century B.C. at the command of the politician Marcus Tullius and is characterized by a pronaos embellished with elegant columns placed above a staircase.

In the cella at one time were several statues, including one in honour of the Emperor Augustus.

58 HOUSE OF THE BLACK WALL

An elegant and refined dwelling characterised by a magnificent decoration on a black background - hence its name - with small painted putti representing *Cupids*. The peristyle is very elegant and distinguished by columns decorated with plaster.

59 HOUSE OF THE FIGURED CAPITALS

This belonged to a noble family. Its construction dates back to the Samnite epoch, as can be appreciated

*Temple of **Fortuna Augusta**: the building was constructed in the imperial age.*

Modesto's Bakery: one of the best-known and largest in Pompeii.

by the sober and severe architectural design.

Of particular interest are the sculptures of the capitals which are now housed in the Pompeii Museum. These depicted "*Bacchic scenes*".

Also worthy of mention is the Lararium and the sundial in the garden.

60 HOUSE OF ARIADNE

This is one of the oldest houses in Pompeii. Here it is possible to admire some fine painted capitals - for this reason the dwelling also bears the name of **House of the Coloured Capitals** - as well as various other paintings executed in the Roman age and belonging to the IV style.

61 HOUSE OF THE HUNT

Constructed in the Samnite epoch, as witnessed by the architecture as a whole and the choice of materials - worthy of particular notice is the tuff façade - it is a noble house and severe in its design. It houses precious pictorial works reproducing for the most part "*Mythological scenes and characters*" and several "**Hunting scenes**" which are particularly delightful. The paintings in the tablinium with a mythological subject have been transferred to the Museum in Naples.

62 MODESTO'S BAKERY

This workshop contains mills for grinding grain - there are four very large ones just in front of the building, - a flour store and a counter used for sales purposes. Here many loaves of bread were found which are now exhibited in the Pompeii Museum.

63 HOUSE OF THE HANGING BALCONY

It stands in the lane which takes its name from the house. It is a truly delightful dwelling and especially interesting for the balcony which adorns the façade. The terrace is a recurrent feature in the architecture of Pompeii and it is widely found in the area of the New Excavations especially.

64 BROTHEL

The word "lupanare" was used to indicate the houses of pleasure. The name derives from "lupa", the term used to define the woman who would call down to the men below and lure them upstairs to where she was waiting. There were various brothels in Pompeii, but this is the largest. It is a building on two floors characterized by lugubrious, small rooms and also includes a waiting room and a latrine. The beds in the *cubicula* are made of stone. The walls are covered in writing and scenes showing amorous embraces. It offers a realistic image of the social life of the time and completes the picture of a city in its many guises.

VI Itinerary: From Via Stabiana to the Porta di Nola

65 Central Thermal Baths - 66 House of Marcus Lucretius - 67 Mill and Bakery - 68 House of the Silver Wedding
69 House of the Centenary - 70 House of Lucretius Fronto - 71 House of the Gladiators - 72 Porta di Nola.

65 CENTRAL THERMAL BATHS

This magnificent complex was constructed immediately after the earthquake of 62 A.D. (in fact many of the materials used were plundered from nearby buildings) and was interrupted as a result of the eruption in 79 A.D. It was built on more modern and functional lines than the Stabian Baths, and had to

answer, given the dramatic population increase, to the growing needs of the citizens. These are in fact bigger than all the other baths - they occupy the area of an entire insula - and are equipped with a large gymnasium, numerous baths and a room intended exclusively as a "sudatorium". The decoration is of the richest and most magnificent appearance.

The principal feature of these Baths

is the way in which their architectural design differs: they were in fact designed to be more spacious compared with the previous ones and, thanks to the large windows which open out (calidarium), are much lighter. In addition the division between the female and male sections was done away with.

66 HOUSE OF MARCUS LUCRETIUS

It belonged to a notable of Pompeii who held, among others, the office of priest of Mars. It is an elegant construction whose rooms were finely decorated with pictures now housed in the Museum in Naples. Those remaining show decorations with imaginary architectural buildings, as well as **Mythological scenes**, depictions of "**Cupids**" and a large painting representing "**Bacchus**". There is a charming garden area, raised compared with the rest of the house, and embellished with statues, niches and fountains.

67 MILL AND BAKERY

The mill, or *pistrinum*, is equipped with all the tools necessary for the grinding of grain, the kneading of dough and therefore the preparation of bread. The visitor can observe the construction system and the workings of the large **grindstones**: these were made up of a fixed base and a revolving upper part: the grain was poured inside and ground by turning the upper part of the mill, either by human strength or with mules.

68 HOUSE OF THE SILVER WEDDING

The house takes its name from the fact that the remains were brought to light on the occasion of the silver wedding of the royal family (1893). It is one of the finest examples of a gentleman's residence: the archi-

House of Marcus Lucretius: a view of the original, elegant garden.

House of the Silver Wedding, a splendid example of a noble house of the imperial age.

tectural design is extremely sober and classical, the decoration magnificent. Executed in the Samnite epoch, it was renovated in the early 1st century A.D. Worthy of particular attention is the atrium consisting of a colonnade of the Corinthian order, grandiose in proportions and soaring dynamically upwards.

Worthy of note are the rooms which flank the peristyle: these offer examples of decoration in the II style. The exedra is elegantly ornamented with festoons; another room shows the original barrel ceilings.

69 HOUSE OF THE CENTENARY

This is one of the largest of the houses among those excavated in Pompeii, being made up of several houses merged into one, which gives it an extremely complex structure. Brought to light on the occasion of the centenary of the eruption of Vesuvius - hence its name - it shows several styles, both in its architecture and in its decoration, indicative of the various building phases.

As well as remembering the "**The young Satyr with wineskins**", a statuette housed in the Archaeological Museum in Naples, worthy of mention are the decoration of the colonnade on a yellow background with the depictions of several *divinities* and *floral motifs* which embellish the two rooms next to the tablinium and the peristyle with a series of decorative motifs consisting of fish and birds.

The peristyle was also furnished with a pool and fountains.

70 HOUSE OF LUCRETIUS FRONTO

It is one of the most elegant and well-balanced dwellings in Pompeii. It is of modest dimensions, but the rooms are harmonious and the decoration of the various rooms extremely refined.

Let us mention among the numerous works present, a series of pictures showing delightful *"landscape views"*, the depiction of *"Venus"*, *"Mars"* and *"Bacchus"*, *"Narcissus gazing at his reflection in the spring"*, *"Theseus and Ariadne"* and *"Venus bathing"*. The large fresco in the garden portrays *"African-type flora and fauna"*.

71 HOUSE OF THE GLADIATORS

This is an actual gladiators' barracks. When the gymnasium in Pompeii was specially built for them to train in, this building was used to provide accommodation for their families. Of interest are the numerous inscriptions found on the columns, all concerning the gladiatorial games and some providing a record of their successes.

72 PORTA DI NOLA

It is one of the eastern gates of the city and is designed with a single arch. Beyond it begins the cemetery area in which the recent excavation works have brought to light various sepulchres and funeral monuments.

House of Marcus Lucretius Fronto: fresco depicting the Wedding of Venus and Mars.

The itinerary includes part of the VI region and is certainly one of the most interesting, since it includes a complex of dwellings of incredible beauty and especially renowned for their extremely refined decoration.

The area lies between Via di Mercurio, the northern boundary wall, Via del Vesuvio and Via della Fortuna.

73 FORUM THERMAL BATHS

These were established in the 1st century B.C. under Sulla and were the only ones still in use after the earthquake of 62 A.D. They include two sections, a male and a female one, both divided into "frigidarium", "tepidarium" and "calidarium". The heating and cooling system of the rooms was achieved by running pipes through the cavities in the walls. All the rooms are elegantly decorated. In the male section - this is the better preserved part - the rooms used for changing are recognizable, as is the *frigidarium* with its circular plan enlivened by large niches (it is embellished with stuccos and paintings); in the *tepidarium* a magnificent barrel vault worked in plaster and a series of telamons (statues leaning against pillars) interspersed with rectangular niches can be admired; finally, the *calidarium* is barrel-vaulted with an apse at the back. The part of the building which looks out onto the street contains workshops.

The Forum Thermal Baths: apodyterium in the baths with the impressions of people taken by surprise at the moment of the eruption.

View of one of the inner rooms of the Baths: the calidarium, the large apsed room used for steam baths at a high temperature.

74 HOUSE OF THE FAUN

It is a dwelling of remarkable proportions, harmonious and well-balanced in its design and elegantly decorated in its various rooms. It represents the classical type of Roman house. It undoubtedly belonged to one of the most prominent local figures, that is the nephew of Sulla who dealt with the political organization of the city.

Its original structure dates back to the Samnite period, that is to the 5th century B.C.; its present-day condition should be dated to the transformations of the 2nd century B.C. The Tuscan atrium belongs to the first period and has a stone floor. The second atrium is, on the other hand, of the Hellenistic type and has four Corinthian columns.

Its reputation and its name are linked essentially to the small bronze of the "**Dancing Faun**" found here, a small masterpiece of ancient statuary. Not to be forgotten, however, is the mosaic housed in the Archaeological Museum in Naples showing the "**Battle of Alexander**", exceptional in terms of its size - it does in fact measure 3.5 m x 6 m - but also in its expressive power: it shows a throng of soldiers, lances and horses captured at the moment when Alexander, by now the victor and proud of his troops, is just about to inflict the decisive blow on the routed enemy. This mosaic paved the tablinium. Among the rooms particularly worthy of mention are the two peristyles: the first has an Ionic colonnade partly decorated with stuccos and with a magnificent exedra, which is also decorated with mosaics, the subject being "**flora and fauna from the Nile region**". The second, the larger of the two, has a Doric colonnade disposed around the garden.

Reconstruction of the House of the Faun.
Opposite above: *House of the Faun: the bronze statue of the dancing Faun, whose original is housed in the Archaeological Museum in Naples.*
Opposite below: *panoramic glimpse of the atrium where the bronze statue of the Faun stands.*

The dancing Faun: one of the most valuable examples of Pompeian statuary.
Above right: detail of the House of the Faun.
Below right: the Battle of Alexander, a large and splendid mosaic now housed in the Archaeological Museum in Naples.

75 HOUSE OF THE GOLDEN CUPIDS

This particularly sumptuous and elegant dwelling belonged to the Poppei family. Its state of preservation allows for particular appreciation of the pictorial complex as well as of the well-balanced and harmonious architectural layout.

It takes its name from the decoration depicting "**Cupids**" situated in one of the cubicula: the graceful figures are painted on gold leaf. A fairly recurrent feature in this house is the presence of theatrical masks.

The peristyle - perhaps the most beautiful part of the house -is partly raised and almost takes the form of a stage: this reveals a certain tendency by the owner to search for new and effective solutions which, however, are not lacking in sobriety and elegance. This space was perhaps intended for theatrical representations, as can be inferred from the presence of a flight of steps and three entrances.

Worthy of note is the decoration of several rooms, for the most part belonging to the III style, and having as their subject "*Mythological episodes and characters*".

Among the curiosities present worthy of mention are the temple dedicated to the cult of the Egyptian goddess Isis - very rarely found in Roman society -, one dedicated to the cult of the Lares and finally the remains of an obsidian mirror.

House of the Golden Cupids: the name derives from the depiction of golden Cupids situated in one of the cubicula.
House of the Vettii: a view of the peristyle restored to its antique splendour by a skilful craftsman.

76 HOUSE OF THE VETTII

This provides a very precious record of Pompeian painting and is one of the most beautiful and interesting houses in the town. The excellent state of preservation allows us, from a distance of centuries, to appreciate the magnificence attained by the dwellings belonging to the most well-to-do class in Pompeii and to observe how the rich local middle-class tended to display their prestige and their high standard of living by their extravagant construction of sumptuous buildings, equal, if not superior, in terms of decorative richness, to those of the aristocracy.

The house of the Vettii, belonged to Aulus Vettius Restitutus and to Aulus Vettius Conviva, and expresses as few others do, the economic position which they had attained at the end of the 1st century A.D. Ac-

tually, the execution of a large part of the pictorial decoration, a dazzling testimony of painting in the IV style, should be attributed to the period after the earthquake of 62 A.D.

We shall now examine in greater detail the various rooms and their painting cycles. The dwelling has remained virtually intact, or has been minutely renovated, and this contributes to the unforgettable atmosphere and impression of stepping back into the past.

In the entrance is "**Priapus**", a very common pornographic figure in Pompeian houses, in that it symbolized fertility, but most importantly served to ward off evil influences from the house.

The decoration of the Atrium - here there are two safes where the owners kept their valuables - takes for its subject "**Cupids**" and "**Psyche**".

The roof has been completely re-

built so as to recreate the most accurate picture possible of that time, as well as a highly evocative atmosphere.

The rooms which open off the atrium contain paintings showing *mythological scenes*, some of which are very interesting in terms of their expressive immediacy.

There is a magnificent peristyle, which skilful renovation has restored to its original form, even as far as the vegetation which characterized it is concerned. It is a precious complex in terms of charm and the admirable fusion of architectural, sculptural and pictorial, as well as naturalistic, features.

The triclinium is the room which has become quite rightly famous for its paintings. The latter, which almost entirely cover the walls (one part has been lost) are on a red background and the depictions are incorporated into mock panels. The

Above: **One of the charming statues which adorn the house.**
Below: **Casa dei Vettii (House of the Vettii): wall frescoes.**
Opposite: **A delightful corner of the House of the Vettii.**

large scenes reproduce mythological characters. "**Perseus and Andromeda**", "**Ariadne and Dionysus**", "**Daphne and Apollo**" and "**Neptune and Amymone**". Of particular interest is the long frieze which runs round the perimeter of the walls: it contains depictions in miniature depicting "**Cupids intent on various activities**", and is of the most refined workmanship.

Let us look at them in detail: "*Cupids at target practice, Cupids with garlands of flowers, Cupids selling perfumes, Cupids with chariots, goldsmith Cupids, Cupids manufacturing cloth, Cupids celebrating sacred rites, Cupids gathering grapes, Cupids celebrating Bacchus and Cupids selling wine*". The large fascia lower down bears depictions of "*Psyche*" intent on weaving garlands of flowers and "*Mythological scenes*".

Other rooms show precious pictorial decoration, for the most part belonging to the IV style. A room in the east section contains pictures representing "*Daedalus and Pasiphae*" and "*Ixion being tortured*", together with large fascias decorated with marine flora and fauna. In another room in the same section there are paintings on mock architecture enclosing depictions of "*Hercules killing the serpent*", the "*Torture of Dirce*" and the "*Torment of Pentheus*".

Of novel interest are the servants' quarters and the kitchen in particular which allow for a reconstruction of domestic life.

Following pages: *Casa dei Vettii (House of the Vettii): the torture of Dirce and Hercules killing the python.*
Opposite: *depiction of Priapus.*
Erotic frescoed scenes in one of the cubicula.
House of the Vettii: the frescos which decorate the Temple of the Lares.

House of the Vettii:
Opposite: *frieze of the Cupids; Wine-making Cupids; Goldsmith Cupids.*
Above: *detail of the frieze of the Cupids.*

Opposite: *One of the very fine friezes which adorn the House of the Vettii.*
House of the Labyrinth: the building belongs to the Samnite period and was decorated with paintings in the II style.

77 HOUSE OF THE LABYRINTH

This house, which takes its name from the subject of the mosaic "*Theseus in the labyrinth*" - dates back to the Samnite period, as can be inferred from the style and from the Tuscan atrium in particular. Another atrium, the one which opens out after the entrance to no.10, is tetrastyle. The pictorial decoration is very fine. That on the walls in the reception area is particularly outstanding and provides, perhaps, one of the most important examples of painting in the II style, characterized by admirably executed mock architecture. In the course of the renovations undergone over the years, the house was equipped with a system of private baths and its own shop for the grinding of grain and for the baking of bread.

78 HOUSE OF APOLLO

The structure and the materials used bear witness to the fact that this dwelling belongs to the most ancient type and that, at a later stage, it was embellished with decorations in the IV style. The name derives from the depictions of "*Apollo and Marsyas*" which decorate the walls of a cubiculum where mock buildings reminiscent of the structure of a theatre can also be found. Of interest are the mosaics situated outside the above-mentioned room and those which once embellished the fountain.

79 HOUSE OF MELEAGER

This was built in the Samnite epoch, but transformed, especially as far as the decorative part is concerned, in

the following era. Worthy of attention is the room used for receptions, characterized by an elegant colonnade with Corinthian capitals. There is also a delightful peristyle with a colonnade which follows the perimeter of the central pool.

80 HOUSE OF ADONIS

It takes its name from the marvellous painting entitled "*Adonis wounded*" which is one of the most beautiful and interesting examples of ancient painting.
It occupies one of the garden walls and is incorporated in the midst of paintings of a landscape nature. Other paintings depicting "*The Toilet of Hermaphroditus*" decorate one of the rooms looking out onto the same garden.

81 HOUSE OF CASTOR AND POLLUX

The dwelling consists of a number of smaller houses, renovated at one time or another, merged into one. Of noteworthy interest is the atrium where a magnificent colonnade with Corinthian columns stands out, as does the pictorial decoration of several rooms, including the series of pictures with mythological scenes depicting "**Apollo and Daphne**", "**Adonis**", "**Silenus**" and "**Scylla**".

The House of Castor and Pollux or of the Dioscuri, owes its name to the depiction of the "**Dioscuri**" which decorated the entrance and which is now housed in the National Museum in Naples, together with other paintings which embellished the other rooms.

82 CAUPONA IN VIA MERCURIO

This is a type of bar-restaurant. The room immediately calls to mind moments of everyday life in ancient Pompeii, thanks above all to the freshness and spontaneity of certain small pictures which are found inside and which, with extreme simplicity, offer a glimpse of the activity involved in this business and the life of the past.

83 HOUSE OF THE SMALL FOUNTAIN AND HOUSE OF THE LARGE FOUNTAIN

Both have a **fountain**, absolute masterpieces of the mosaic art.

House of the Large Fountain: detail of one of the mosaics inside.
Opposite: *House of the Large Fountain: detail of the nymphaeum with its elegant and precious mosaic decoration.*

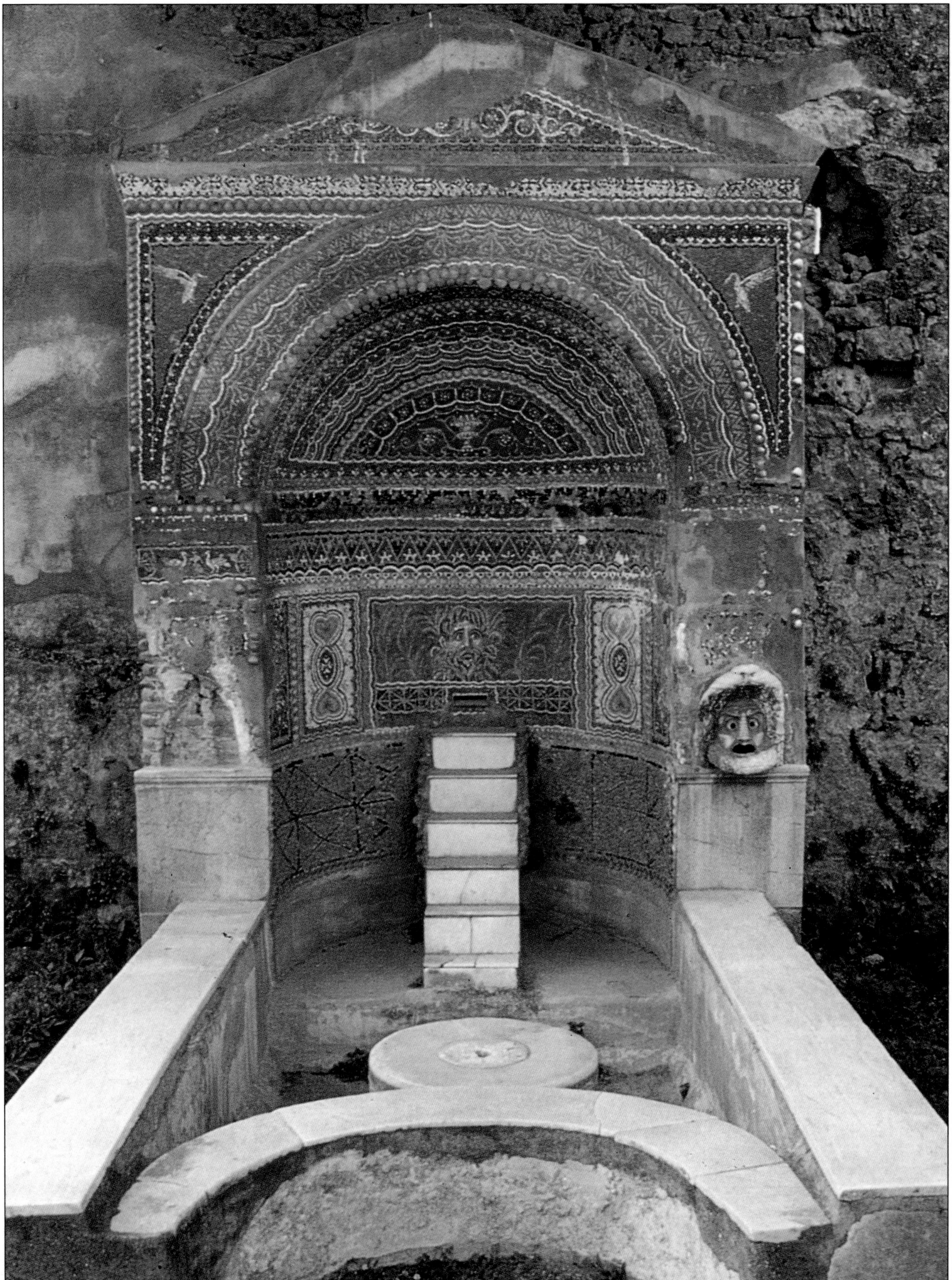

The one in the House of the Large Fountain consists of a niche which is completely covered with polychrome tesserae. It is embellished with a bronze statue and theatrical masks.

These nymphaea, made of glass paste stones, are rare examples of non-floor mosaics.

Of additional interest is the pictorial decoration in the first of the two houses, which contains some delightful small pictures inspired by the landscape.

84 ARCH OF CALIGULA

This stands at the crossroads which forms the junction of Via del Foro, Via delle Terme, Via della Fortuna and Via del Mercurio: it provides access to the latter.

Arch of Caligula: it was built at the crossroads of the most important thoroughfares of Pompeii.

VIII Itinerary: From the Forum to Porta Ercolano to Villa of the Mysteries

85 House of the Tragic Poet - 86 House of Pansa - 87 House of Sallust - 88 House of the Surgeon - 89 Porta Ercolano

90 Via dei Sepolcri and Sepulchres - 91 Villa of the Mosaic Columns - 92 Villa of Diomedes - 93 Villa of the Mysteries.

85 HOUSE OF THE TRAGIC POET

Its name derives from the mosaic scene depicting a "**Master of the theatre**". It dates back to the imperial age and is luxurious and refined, especially in terms of the fine decoration of some of the rooms. The architectural design is composite and harmonious: it is of modest but well-balanced proportions. The presence of workshops adjacent to the dwelling leads us to suppose that the owner was involved in commerce. At the entrance is the characteristic "*cave canem*" (beware of the dog), one of the best-known images from Pompeii. The depiction of the "*tragic poet*" was found in the tablinium and has given its name to the dwelling and several paintings. The series of paintings in the triclinium take as their subject scenes from mythology: T*heseus and* A*riadne* and V*enus and cupids*. Other paintings with a mythological subject decorate the walls of the cubicula.

There is a very fine fresco showing the "**Sacrifice of Iphigenia**" housed in the Archaeological Museum in Naples. Some experts have identified it as a copy of the work by the famous Greek painter Timante of the 5th century B.C.

86 HOUSE OF PANSA

A building of vast proportions, to the extent that it alone occupies the whole of insula no. 6. The original structure dates back to the Samnite period. Subsequently the dwelling was subdivided into a series of small rooms intended to be let, as is proved by an inscription to this effect and by the presence of an independent entrance to each of these small apartments.

This conversion of the building is proof of the changing needs of Pompeian society which, in the 1st

---

House of the Tragic Poet: in the entrance is the well-known depiction of the "cave canem" (beware of the dog) in mosaic.

House of Pansa: overall view of the area of the peristyle.

century A.D., passed from being a primarily agricultural economy - the inhabitants of the houses were land-owners, as is indicated by the presence of the plot of land behind the house - to one based on enterprise and commerce. There is a beautiful Tuscan atrium (it is part of the original construction) and a peristyle which is laid out around a pool. Behind it open out the rooms set aside for service purposes, in-cluding kitchens, latrines and a building for housing vehicles as well as the area intended for use as a vegetable garden.

The original decoration has been completely lost.

87 HOUSE OF SALLUST

An interesting construction of the Samnite epoch, as demonstrated by the Tuscan atrium with its jutting out roof sloping towards the impluvium to facilitate the collection of rainwater. The decoration is primarily in the form of plaster coverings and belongs to the I style.

Some rooms show evidence of renovations and paintings of a period subsequent to the date of construction. One such example of this is the fresco depicting the myth of **Actaeon assailed by dogs** which adorned the garden.

88 HOUSE OF THE SURGEON

Its name derives from the series of surgical instruments found here which are now housed in the Archaeological Museum in Naples, and the nature of which leads us to suppose that a doctor lived here.

The structure corresponds to the type of the oldest houses in Pompeii, both as regards the architectural design, the distribution of the rooms, and the materials used in its construction (4th-3rd century B.C.). The simple and severe façade is covered with stone slabs.

89 PORTA ERCOLANO

It has three arches, two of which were reserved for pedestrians. Its construction dates back to the Roman age, but another much simpler gate previously existed on the site. Opening onto the north-eastern stretch of the city walls, it also provided the most important access to Pompeii. Its other name was Porta Saliensis, in memory of the fact that it was from here that the carts transporting salt used to travel.

90 VIA DEI SEPOLCRI AND SEPULCHRES

Along the Via dei Sepolcri is a vast cemetery area which is the most impressive and the most important of all those which stood on the outskirts of the city. The feature of greatest importance is the presence of a complex of dwellings, villas and workshops which, in terms of number and quality, constitute a real town centre. This feature confirms the enormous expansion which Pompeii underwent at the height of its splendour, to the extent that suburbs, which were well organized from every standpoint, sprang up outside the traditional boundary wall. As a consequence, this section of the city can also be said to have played a role of primary importance, both from the historical-social and from the urbanistic point of view. The street, apart from villas such as those belonging to Diomedes and to Cicero, and the one known as the Villa of the Mosaic Columns, is also flanked by numerous workshops.

THE SEPULCHRES

They are of various types and forms: small temples and exedrae, altars or honorary cippi and mau-

Via dei Sepolcri and view of some of the funeral monuments along it.
Via dei Sepolcri: glimpse of the necropolis area and the funeral monuments along the road.

soleums. Funeral collections and decorations of artistic merit have been found in many of these. Among the most interesting and outstanding sepulchres are: the sepulchre of the *priestess* M*amia*, that of the I*stacides* (characterised by a raised temple on a podium), that of T*erentius* M*aior*, of the so-called "*blue vase*" (so-called after the magnificent vase found here and now housed in the Museum in Naples), that of U*mbricius* S*caurus* (it shows admirable depictions of "gladiator games"). Each sepulchre, be it large or small, bears the name of the deceased or of the family which owned it. Often their business is indicated and the event which made them famous is commemorated.

91 VILLA OF THE MOSAIC COLUMNS

This takes its name from the magnificent and original columns covered with mosaics found here during the excavation works. These can be admired in the Archaeological Museum in Naples. There is a beautiful mosaic fountain adorning the garden.

92 VILLA OF DIOMEDES

Here we have before us one of the masterpieces of Pompeian architecture, especially in terms of the unusual design of the building. Indeed, though it maintains certain

important features of the Roman-type house, it is laid out with an eye for space and light and above all is spread over various floors, following the natural inclination of the terrain, resulting in the building being constructed in an airier and more original way. This residence, situated along the Via dei Sepolcri, is of vast proportions. The principal nucleus is that of the equally enormous garden, surrounded by a long colonnade which creates a porticoed space, furnished with a pool. The rooms lie on one side of the garden itself and are arranged in their turn around a peristyle which communicates directly with the outside. Worthy of particular attention is the large apsed room, character-

Villa of Diomedes: one of the luxury suburban dwellings.

Villa of Diomedes: the construction is of vast proportions: there is a magnificent garden and the construction of the rooms is well-designed.

ized by its airiness and the wide-ranging view which it enjoys. There is a beautiful open gallery which also shares views of the gulf, as does the terrace, which at one time lay along the whole length of the colonnade. At the corner of the entrance to the villa are the baths furnished with a small pool. A series of little steps links the staggered floors to one another, creating further interest.

One of these staircases leads to the cryptoporticus, that is to say the underground rooms of the dwelling. Eighteen bodies were found in this house, a further proof of the disaster which struck Pompeii in 79 A.D. The villa was brought to light in the second half of the 1700s and thought - though in an arbitrary way - to be the house of Arrius Diomedes because it was situated opposite his tomb.

93 VILLA OF THE MYSTERIES

This villa stands right on the outskirts of Pompeii, beyond the archaeological area proper.

Grandiose in its proportions and famous for its magnificent fresco cycle, it has, since the discovery of the first rooms, created great excitement among the experts owing not only to its complexity and the special nature of its architectural design, but above all for the precious pictorial cycle and for the interpretation of the latter, connected with the religious cults which existed alongside the official religion.

The villa was built around the 2nd century B.C., but was renovated and embellished in the imperial age, an epoch in which it assumed the splendid appearance which is still recognisable today, even if somewhat impoverished by the loss of certain furnishings and many precious ornaments as a consequence of the earthquake of 62 A.D. when it was abandoned by its owner.

THE ARCHITECTURAL DESIGN.

The villa has a square plan. To make it conform to the irregular and uneven terrain on the site, unlike the villa of Diomedes which overcame the problem by means of a complex organization of its structure and linking stairways, the Villa of the Mysteries was supported on a base created on a specially made embankment, so that the whole house could lie on a single level and thus be constructed in a very regular and well-balanced way. In addition a long colonnade and a series of gardens unite the building with its surrounding environment, creating a truly delightful and harmonious whole. The entrance to the villa is through an exedra, a sort of bright veranda open towards the

Villa of the Mysteries: view of the outside, constructed on staggered levels.

Villa of the Mysteries: the interior.

outside, either side of which are two "viridaria" (terraces with garden) and two colonnades. The tablinium and the atrium follow: the first contains a splendid pictorial decoration on a black background and delicate miniatures (III style). The cubicula, the rooms next to the atrium, contain magnificent decorations in the II style with daring use of perspective. On the part at the back an airy peristyle opens up with sixteen Doric columns. Beyond it are the courtyard and the service rooms. The villa is equipped with two ovens and rooms for wine-making. Several rooms are furnished with bathing facilities.

The pictorial cycle: "Cycle of the Mysteries"

The first impression gained on entering this room is one of sheer amazement. The walls are covered with an absolute masterpiece of painting: life-size figures tower up in the frescos and the outstanding use of that shade of "*red*" known as "Pompeian" admirably unifies the various scenes. The long line of depictions unravels freely without any break in continuity. Although at first it might be impossible to grasp the meaning behind the paintings, they reveal a sense of something great and mysterious all the same.

Although the experts do not all agree on their interpretation of the meaning of the "cycle of the Mysteries", fundamentally they all recognize it as referring to the initiation rites to the Mysteries of the cult of Dionysus. This cult was forbidden by the Roman government because it was thought to bring about disorder and considered to be remote from the state religion, though it was especially deeply-rooted in south Italy, where it was easier to escape the watchful eye of the Eternal City. The cycle of paintings in the villa must therefore be seen not only as an important record of pictorial art, but also as an exceptional proof of the survival, in the suburbs, of the Dionysiac rites.

The scenes shown in this room - we shall go by the interpretation which has gained most consensus among the experts who have tackled the problem - probably depict the initiation rites at the wedding of a bride, probably the lady of the house, identified by some as the veiled figure in one of the panels.

Reconstruction of the narrative journey: 1st scene: T*he young Dionysus reads the sacred ritual, while a seated woman listens and another standing follows the reading*:

2nd scene: *a young girl bears offerings; a seated woman, helped by two youths, purifies herself;*

3rd scene: *Silenus plays the lyre, while a woman offers milk to a fawn;*

4th scene: *a terrified girl takes flight*

Opposite: *the frescos showing "the initiation into the Dionysiac rites".*

(notice the cloak which billows up owing to the young woman's haste);

5th scene: *Silenus offers water to a young Satyr, while another holds up above him a theatrical mask;*

6th scene: *the wedding ceremony of Dionysus and Ariadne;*

7th scene: *a woman keeps hidden behind a cloth the symbol of fertility, while a winged figure strikes with a whip a young woman who is leaning on another's lap* (the flagellation was part of the rite of initiates);

8th scene: *the dance of a Bacchante;*

9th scene: *the future bride prepares for the rite;*

10th scene: *a seated woman observes the whole scene;* this is perhaps the portrait of the lady of the house, she herself an initiate in the Dionysiac rite.

Regardless of the meaning of the individual depictions, what is most striking is the masterful orchestration of the whole and the narrative capacity of this unknown artist, who, with skilful conciseness and a strong pictorial sense, has succeeded in rendering in an admirable way the mysterious atmosphere which governed the rites of the god. The density of colours and the ceaseless flow of the figures, as well as the balanced formulation of the whole cycle, make it an unforgettable masterpiece. The rooms in the rest of the villa are decorated with paintings in the II style. The section which contains the kitchens, baths and storehouses is worth a visit, as is the cryptoporticus where small and narrow windows create a unique contrast between darkness and light. Many corpses were found in the villa, taken by surprise during the appalling tragedy. The statue of Livia which is now housed in the Antiquarium in Pompeii was also found here.

Below: *Cycle of the Mysteries: the reading of the ritual*
Opposite: *flagellation of a woman and dance of the Bacchante.*

Cycle of the Mysteries: a Silenus offers water to a Satyr.
Cycle of the Mysteries: the uncovering of Dionysus' phallus.
Opposite: Cycle of the Mysteries: a child reads the ritual.